U0925178

最深刻的思想或感情就如同地底的矿藏，在等待着同样深沉的
头脑与心灵去发现和开采。

The profoundest thought or passion sleeps as in a mine until an equal mind and heart finds and publishes it.

那些激励我前行的睿思

张　露／编译

江苏人民出版社

图书在版编目（CIP）数据

那些激励我前行的睿思：英汉对照 / 张露编译. -- 南京：江苏人民出版社，2016.1
ISBN 978-7-214-12874-4

Ⅰ. ①那… Ⅱ. ①张… Ⅲ. ①英语—汉语—对照读物 Ⅳ. ① H319.4

中国版本图书馆 CIP 数据核字（2015）第 315021 号

书　　名	那些激励我前行的睿思：英汉对照
编 译 者	张　露
责任编辑	朱　超
装帧设计	浪殿设计　飞　扬
版式设计	张文艺
出版发行	凤凰出版传媒股份有限公司 江苏人民出版社
出版社地址	南京市湖南路1号A楼，邮编：210009
出版社网址	http://www.jspph.com http://jsrmcbs.tmall.com
经　　销	凤凰出版传媒股份有限公司
印　　刷	北京中印联印务有限公司
开　　本	718 毫米 ×1000 毫米 1/16
印　　张	12
字　　数	129 千字
版　　次	2016 年 5 月第 1 版　2016 年 5 月第 1 次印刷
标准书号	978-7-214-12874-4
定　　价	24.00元

The Thoughts Inspiring My Soul

那些激励我前行的睿思

目 录 | CONTENTS

心灵的美誉芳醇

生命不在于完成

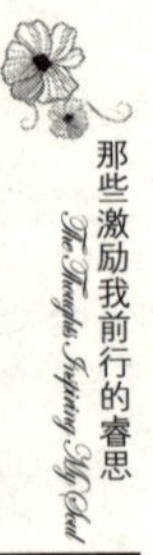

CONTENTS 目录

活出最真的自我

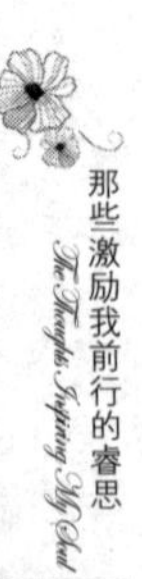

成长在灵魂高处

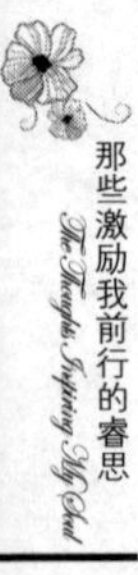

Chapter 1

心灵的美誉芳醇

Distrust can be contagious. But, so can trust.

——Robbins Stacia

不信任有传染性。但是信任也如此。

——斯达卡

论爱情

◎ Francis Bacon

The stage is more beholding to love, than the life of man. For as to the stage, love is ever matter of comedies, and now and then of tragedies; but in life it doth much **mischief**① ; sometimes like a siren, sometimes like a fury.

You may observe, that amongst all the great and worthy persons (whereof the memory remaineth, either ancient or recent) there is not one, that hath been transported to the mad degree of love: which shows that great spirits, and great business, do keep out this weak passion. You must except, nevertheless, Marcus Antonius, the half partner of the empire of Rome, and Appius Claudius, the decemvir and lawgiver; whereof the former was indeed a **voluptuous**② man, and inordinate; but the latter was an austere and wise man: and therefore it seems (though rarely) that love can find entrance, not only into an open heart, but also into a heart well fortified, if watch be not well kept.

① mischief ['mɪstʃɪf] n. 损害，危害；顽皮，淘气；恶作剧；祸根

② voluptuous [və'lʌptʃuəs] adj. 性感的；令人感到舒适的，倾向感官享受的；骄奢淫逸的

作者简介

弗朗西斯·培根（Francis Bacon，1561—1626），英国文艺复兴时期最重要的散作家，唯物主义哲学家，科学家。被马克思称为“英国唯物主义和整个现代实验科学的真正始祖”。代表作《新工具》《学术的进步》《新大西岛》等。

相比生活，爱情更偏爱舞台。因为在舞台上，爱情总是喜剧，偶尔掺杂着悲剧；可在生活中，就非常麻烦了：生活中的爱情时而充满诱惑，时而让人愤怒。

你可以观察一下，所有伟人之中（古往今来，凡记忆所到之处）竟无一人为爱疯狂。这就说明了，凡是伟大的精神、伟大的事业，都将这脆弱的激情隔绝在外。然而，肯定也有例外，罗马帝国的半友人马可·奥勒利乌斯，古罗马行政官兼立法者克劳狄乌斯，就是例外：前者本是骄奢淫逸之人；后者却严谨而明智。由此可知，好像（尽管很少）爱情总能找到入口，它不仅能进入敞开的心扉，还能钻进城墙高筑却疏于守备的心门。

伊壁鸠鲁有云，人生不过是一座大戏台；好像为天国之冥思而生的人类，以及一切高贵的事物，都该抛开一切拜倒在一尊小小的神像前，

It is a poor saying of Epicurus, Satis magnum alter alteri theatrum sumus; as if man, made for the contemplation of heaven, and all noble objects, should do nothing but kneel be-fore a little idol, and make himself a subject, though not of the mouth (as beasts are), yet of the eye; which was given him for higher purposes.

It is a strange thing, to note the excess of this passion, and how it braves the nature, and value of things, by this; that the speaking in a **perpetual**① hyper-bole, is comely in nothing but in love. Neither is it merely in the phrase; for whereas it hath been well said, that the arch-flatterer, with whom all the petty flatterers have intelligence, is a man's self; certainly the lover is more. For there was never proud man thought so absurdly well of him-self, as the lover doth of the person loved; and therefore it was well said, that it is impossible to love, and to be wise. Neither doth this weakness appear to others only, and not to the party loved; but to the loved most of all, except the love be reciproque. For it is a true rule, that love is ever re-warded, either with the reciproque, or with an inward and secret contempt.

By how much the more, men ought to beware of this passion, which loseth not only other things, but itself! As for the other losses, the poet's relation doth well figure them: that he that preferred Helena, quitted the gifts of Juno and Pallas. For whosoever esteemeth too much of amorous affection, quitteth both riches and wisdom.

This passion hath his floods, in very times of weakness; which are great

① perpetual [pə'pɛtʃuəl] adj. 永久的；不断的；无期限的；四季开花的

让自己虽不至屈从于口腹之欲（像野兽一样），却难逃耳目色相之劫；它们本该有更高尚的用途。

因此，要说清这万物的激情和价值，以及它在本性面前是如何无畏无惧，是一件很奇怪的事情；无尽的浮夸，只有在爱情里才显得美妙。这种浮夸不仅在于辞藻，因为有句话说得好，最大的奉承，人总会留给自己；而对爱人的奉承可谓更甚。即便再骄傲的人，也不会像陷入爱河之人迷恋他所爱的人那般迷恋自己；因而有人云，爱情与理智不可兼得。这种缺陷，不仅外人能看到，被爱之人也能看到；而且被爱之人看得最清楚，除非对方也爱上了你。这是一条不争定律，爱本就是付出，要么得到回报，要么被暗自轻蔑。

人们可千万要小心这种情欲，它不仅会使你失去其他东西，还会使你失去它自己！对于所谓的其他东西，诗人早已贴切形容：他选择了海伦娜，就是放弃了朱诺和雅典娜。也就是说，那些太过看重情爱之欲之人，就等于放弃了财富和智慧。

每当人心显露脆弱，这种激情便会涌入；或是春风得意日，或是苦难交加时；尽管后者出现的情况较少，可两种情况都会点燃爱情之火，并让它愈演愈烈，因而就像愚人之子。那些不得不接受爱情的人，仍然

prosperity, and great adversity; though this latter hath been less observed: both which times kindle love, and make it more fervent, and therefore show it to be the child of folly. They do best, who if they cannot but admit love, yet make it keep quarters; and sever it wholly from their serious affairs, and actions, of life; for if it check once with business, it troubleth men's fortunes, and maketh men, that they can no ways be true to their own ends.

I know not how, but martial men are given to love: I think, it is but as they are given to wine; for perils commonly ask to be paid in pleasures.

There is in man's nature, a secret inclination and motion, towards love of others, which if it be not spent upon some one or a few, doth naturally spread itself towards many, and maketh men become humane and charitable; as it is seen sometime in friars.

Nuptial love maketh mankind; friendly love perfecteth it; but wanton love corrupteth, and embaseth it.

尽力约束它，并将它完整地与生活中严肃的事业和行为隔开。因为一旦爱情沾上了事业，就会影响人们的运势，他们就无从实现最终目标。

我不知道为什么，军人总容易深陷爱河。我想，正如他们沉湎于酒一样，因为从事危险的工作总需要欢愉来给予慰藉。

人类的天性之中，本存有对他人的爱之倾向，若这种爱无法给予一个或几个人，那么它很自然地就成了博爱，如此一来，便更显人性与慈悲；正如在修士身上所见。

婚姻之爱，造就人；友谊之爱，升华人；然而荒淫之爱，腐蚀人、摧毁人。

On Pleasure

论快乐

◎ Kahlil Gibran

Pleasure is a freedom song, but it is not freedom. It is the blossoming of your desires, but it is not their fruit; it is depth calling onto a height, but it is not the deep nor the height; it is the caged taking wing, but it is not space encompassed. Ay, in very truth, pleasure is a freedom song. And I fain would have you sing it with fullness of heart; yet I would not have you lose your hearts in the singing.

Some of your youth seek pleasure as if it was all, and they are judged and rebuked. I would not judge nor rebuke them. I would have them seek, for they shall find pleasure, but not her alone; seven are her sisters, and the least of them is more beautiful than pleasure. Have you not heard of the man who was digging in the earth for roots and found a treasure?

And some of your elders remember pleasures with regret like wrongs committed in drunkenness. But the regret is the beclouding of the mind and its chastisement. They should remember their pleasures with gratitude, as they

作者简介

卡里·纪伯伦（Kahlil Gibran，1883—1931），黎巴嫩诗人、作家和画家。被称为“艺术天才”“黎巴嫩文坛骄子”，是阿拉伯现代小说、艺术和散文的主要奠基人，20世纪阿拉伯新文学道路的开拓者之一。作品形散而神不散，是阿拉伯近代文学史上首位使用散文诗体的作家。代表作《我的心灵告诫我》《先知》《论友谊》等。

快乐是一首自由的歌曲，但它又不是自由本身。它是绽放你梦想的花朵，但不是花朵的果实；它是从深谷向高山的呼唤，但不是高低的山峦；它是笼中展翅的鸟儿，却不是困缚的空间。喔，的确，快乐是一首自由之歌。愿你们能够倾心诠释这首歌曲；愿你们不要在歌声中迷失了自己的心。

一些年轻人别无所求，把追寻快感当作生活的全部，他们很快就受到了审判和谴责。但我不会审判和谴责他们。我会让他们去尽情追寻，因为他们会寻找到快乐，而不单单是快感本身；快乐有七个姐妹，最小的妹妹比快乐更加美丽。难道你们没听说过，一个男人在挖树根的时候发现了宝藏的故事吗?

一些年长的人带着遗憾回忆快乐，就像在追忆那些酒醉后犯下的错误。但遗憾只会让心灵蒙上一层阴影，而不是对它的惩戒。他们应带着感恩的心去回忆快乐，就如同回忆盛夏硕果累累的愉悦时刻。但如果后

would the harvest of a summer. Yet if it comforts them to regret, let them be comforted.

And there are among you those who are neither young to seek nor old to remember; and in their fear of seeking and remembering they shun all pleasures, lest they neglect the spirit or offend against it.

But even in their foregoing is their pleasure.

And thus they too find a treasure though they dig for roots with quivering hands.

But tell me, who is he that can offend the spirit?

Shall the nightingale offend the stillness of the night, or the firefly the stars? And shall your flame or your smoke burden the wind?

Think you the spirit is a still pool which you can trouble with a staff? Oftentimes in denying yourself pleasure you do but store the desire in the recesses of your being.

Who knows but that which seem omitted today, waits for tomorrow? Even your body knows its heritage and its rightful need and will not be deceived.

And your body is the harp of your soul, and it is yours to bring forth sweet music from it or confused sounds.

And now you ask in your heart, "How shall we distinguish that which is good in pleasure from that which is not good?" Go to your fields and your gardens and you shall learn that it is pleasure of the bee to gather honey of the flower, but it is also the pleasure of the flower to yield its honey to the bee, for

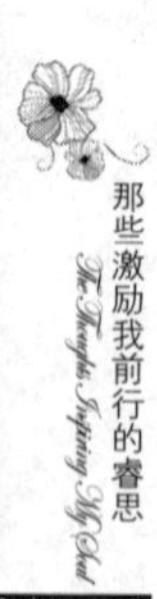

悔能使他们得到心理安慰，那就让他们得到慰藉吧。

还有一些人，过了追梦的年龄，却暂无回忆的沉淀；他们逃避一切追寻快乐和回忆快乐的机会，唯恐忽视或惹恼了心灵。

然而在这样的行径中，也有他们自己的快乐。

因此，即使他们用颤抖的手刨根，也会找到宝藏。

但有谁能告诉我，谁敢惹恼心灵呢?

夜莺会扰乱夜的寂静，萤火虫会惹怒繁星吗? 你们的火焰和烟雾会惊扰风的方向吗?

你们以为心灵就像一汪清泉可以让你们肆意破坏吗? 你们常常表面拒绝快乐，却将对快乐的渴求深埋于心。

可是谁又知道，今天被忽略的事，明天会不会发生呢? 甚至你们的身体也明白它所承存的合理需求，而不会被欺骗。

你们的身体是你们心灵的琴弦，它抑或奏出美妙的乐曲，抑或拨弄出混乱的声响，全取决于你们。

现在，你们问问自己的内心：“我们该如何分辨快乐的真假呢? ”你们去到田野花园瞧瞧便知，快乐就是蜜蜂忙碌于蕊间采蜜，而花朵也乐于将花蜜奉献给蜜蜂，花朵是蜜蜂的生存之基，蜜蜂又是花朵爱的传信

to the bee a flower is a fountain of life, and to the flower a bee is a messenger of love, and to both, bee and flower, the giving and receiving of pleasure is a need and an ecstasy.

People of Orphaless, be in your pleasures like the flowers and the bees.

者，对它们来说，蜜蜂和花朵，给予和接受都是令彼此狂喜的快乐。

奥菲利斯城的人们，请像花朵和蜜蜂一样，尽情享受你们的快乐吧！

Frankness
坦率

◎ Robert E. Lee

You must study to be frank with the world: frankness is the child of honesty and courage. Say just what you mean to do, on every occasion. If a friend asks a favor, you should grant it, if it is reasonable; if not, tell him plainly why you cannot. You would wrong him and wrong yourself by equivocation of any kind.

Never do a wrong thing to make a friend or keep one. The man who requires you to do so is dearly purchased at a sacrifice. Deal kindly but firmly with all your classmates. You will find it the policy which wears best. Above all, do not appear to others what you are not.

If you have any fault to find with any one, tell him, not others, of what you complain. There is no more dangerous experiment than that of undertaking to do one thing before a man's face and another behind his back. We should say and do nothing to the injury of any one. It is not only a matter of principle, but also the path of peace and hornor.

作者简介

罗伯特·爱德华·李（Robert Edward Lee，1807—1870），美国军事家。曾任华盛顿大学校长，并积极从事教育事业，维持着联合国代表象征及重要教育家的形象至今。

你必须学会对这个世界真诚以待：坦率是诚实与勇气之子。在每一个场合，你都要说出自己真实的想法。如果有朋友请你帮忙，只要合情合理，你便该予以帮助；如若不然，就坦白告诉他为什么你不能施以援手。含糊其辞既会委屈自己，也会委屈朋友。

千万不要为了结交朋友或者维持友谊而做错事。对你有如此要求的人终会付出沉痛的代价。对待同学要友善，但也要有原则。你会发现，这是最为实用的准则。最重要的是，不要在他人面前伪装自己。

如果你发现了某人的缺点，就告诉他本人，而不是向他人抱怨。最危险的事情莫过于做人当面一套，背后一套。有损他人的话语我们不能说，伤害他人的事情我们不能做。这不仅是一种做人原则，还是与他人和睦相处、获得他人尊重之道。

Educating Yourself About the Art of Loving
学习爱的艺术

◎ Paul Mauchline

Katherine Anne Porter wrote, "Love must be learned, and learned again and again; there is no end to it." Katherine Anne is right: there is no end to it. Each day, we need to love ourselves. Each day, we need to demonstrate our love for our partner and family, and for all those we encounter. So how do we get to the point where we are able to show our love for others and ourselves every day? I feel that the answer lies in how we view love. In his book published in 1956, The Art of Loving, Erich Fromm describes love as an art that requires effort, knowledge and practice. To view love as an art is to imagine that the capacity for love is a seed that lies within each of us, and that growing that seed is solely our own responsibility.

The practice of any art requires knowledge. **By virtue of**[1] the fact you are reading this article, I assume you are seeking knowledge about the art of loving. Many of us today are reading books by authors like John Gray, Barbara

① by virtue of 由于

凯瑟琳·安·波特写道："爱需要学习，学习，再学习，永无止境。"凯瑟琳·安说得没错，对爱的学习是没有止境的。每天我们都需要爱自己，爱我们的伴侣和家人，还有那些偶遇的人。那么，我们该如何表达对自己和他人的爱呢？我认为，答案取决于我们如何看待爱。埃利希·弗洛姆在 1956 年出版的《爱的艺术》中，把爱描述成一件需要努力、知识和练习的艺术。把爱视为艺术，就好比把爱当成一枚种子，种在我们每个人的心间，我们需要对它负责，让它茁壮成长。

练习任何一门艺术都需要知识。当你在读这篇文章时，我猜你正在寻找和爱的艺术相关的知识。如今，有很多人会阅读像约翰·格雷、芭芭拉·安吉丽思、约翰·布拉德肖、托马斯·摩尔还有其他类似作家的

De Angelis, John Bradshaw, Thomas Moore, and countless others. The reason we are reading is quite simple: we are seeking more knowledge about love and relationships. It's very apparent, from the number of seminars, tapes, videos, and books available, that there is need for this type of knowledge.

Have you attended a seminar or read a book on relationships in the last year? Whether you have, or have not, is not important right now. What is important is that you recognize that knowledge is the first step. Take responsibility for your own education. Participating in a seminar or workshop, reading a book, and even reading this article is a gesture of loving yourself. Just do not forget that knowledge acquisition is a continuous process; it does not stop after one or two seminars, or after reading a few books. It takes effort on your part to gain the knowledge you need. Instead of just sitting watching television, you are reading this article right now, but it does not mean the effort has to end once you finish reading what I have to say here. You just may feel inspired, with new ideas on life, love, and relationships. It's up to you to put in the effort to incorporate these ideas into your life…and to keep them alive. It's not going to be easy—it's going to require hard work and effort. You cannot change life-long habits overnight, after reading one article. Somehow, with the pace of life and the conveniences we now have, we have come to expect things to happen instantly. Improving our relationships and ourselves is about changing old habits, some of which we have had since childhood. These changes do not occur instantly, but require continuous effort over time.

What exactly does "effort" mean, when it comes to loving? In my

书。这些书热门的原因很简单，我们渴望更多关于爱和情感的知识。从相关的研讨会、磁带、视频和书籍的数量中可以很明显地看出，这类知识受到人们的热捧。

去年，你有参加过类似的情感研讨会或是阅读相关的书籍吗？不论有或没有，现在已经无关紧要了。重要的是，你要认识到相关的知识是学习爱的艺术的第一步。从现在起，重视自己的学习，参加一个研讨会或讲习班，阅读一些书籍，甚至是阅读这篇文章，这都是你爱自己的表现。但不要忘记，学习是一个长期的过程，不要只是参加了一两个研讨会，或是读了几本书后就停止学习。想要学习这门艺术，你需要付出很多的努力。你没有坐在电视机前，而是在看这篇文章，这很好，但这并不意味着读完这篇文章后就万事大吉了。你也许会灵光一闪，想到很多有关人生、爱和感情的新的想法。但能否把这些想法融入你的生活，并让它们持续焕发光彩，就要看你自己了。这并不容易，你需要花很多的时间和精力。你不可能在读完这篇文章后，一晚上就改变了你日积月累下养成的习惯。飞快的生活节奏以及现今我们身边的各种便利，让我们总是希望事情一下子就能做好。想改善情感和我们自身，就要改变一些老旧的习惯，有些习惯还是我们从小就养成的。改变习惯不会一蹴而就，而是要长时间不间断地努力。

当爱和努力联系在一起时，努力到底意味着什么？我认为，努力就是时间和行动。你明天早上起床时，问问自己，我今天能更爱自己一点

opinion, effort is time and action. When you get up tomorrow morning, take the time to ask yourself: How can I be more loving to myself today? How can I give more love to my partner? What action can I take to give love today? Use your imagination to come up with creative ways of showing love for yourself and others. Take the time to follow through with your thoughts and put them into action. I am not talking about lavish gifts or tropical holidays; it's the little continuous gestures of love that count. Having a bubble bath, making yourself a special dinner, taking a mental health day from work, sleeping in, taking a drive in the country, spending time at a hobby, curling up with a good book, or even reading material like this or attending a workshop or seminar are gestures of loving yourself. You can give love to your partner in many little ways, too: A telephone call during the day to say, "Hi, how are you? I was thinking about you…", bringing home a single flower or a little gift, going for an evening walk together, giving **spontaneous**① hugs, holding hands, giving a back rub, showering together, reading aloud to one another, or leaving a little love note on the bathroom mirror...the list goes on and on. All it takes is imagination. The possibilities are endless.

We will never know everything. That is the beauty of life, and, more importantly, that is the beauty of love—for they are really both one in the same. Remember it all starts with you. Take the time to expand your knowledge of love, and practice the art of loving, always, to create the loving life you deserve.

---

① spontaneous [spɒn'teɪnɪəs] adj. 自发的；自然的；无意识的

吗？能更爱自己的伴侣吗？我该怎样表达爱？想出一些新颖的方式来向你自己和他人献上爱吧。让你的想法慢慢在头脑里成形，并把它付诸实际。我不会用奢侈的礼物和热带旅游来表达爱，这种爱的表达方式不会长久。爱自己的方法有很多，比如泡泡澡，为自己准备一个特别的晚餐，让自己的精神休息一天，睡个懒觉，在乡边骑自行车，花点时间在自己的兴趣爱好上，读一本好书，甚至是看这篇文章，或是参加讲习班或研讨会。你也可以在很多小事上向你的伴侣表达爱：给他（她）打通电话，关心一下："你好吗，我很想你……"带一支花或是一份小礼物回家，晚上一起出去散步，给一个自然的拥抱，紧紧握住对方的手，给对方做背部按摩，一起淋浴，把一本书的内容大声读给对方听，或是在浴室的镜子上留下一张爱的留言……还有很多很多。你需要想象去做这些事情，要相信，任何奇迹都会发生。

我们难以知晓下一秒会发生什么。这就是生命之美，这更是爱之美，因为它们本来就如出一辙。要知道，一切都因你而改变。花时间去增长你对爱的见解，练习爱的艺术，去塑造你值得拥有的充满爱的人生吧！

论美

◎ Francis Bacon

Virtue is like a rich stone, best plain set; and surely virtue is best, in a body that is comely, though not of delicate features; and that hath rather dignity of presence, than beauty of aspect.

Neither is it almost seen, that very beautiful per-sons are otherwise of great virtue; as if nature were rather busy, not to err, than in labor to produce excellency. And therefore they prove accomplished, but not of great spirit; and study rather behavior, than virtue. But this holds not always: for Augustus Caesar, Titus Vespasianus, Philip le Belle of France, Edward the Fourth of England, Alcibiades of Athens, Ismael the Sophy of Persia, were all high and great spirits; and yet the most beautiful men of their times. In beauty, that of favor, is more than that of color; and that of decent and gracious motion, more than that of favor. That is the best part of beauty, which a picture cannot express; no, nor the first sight of the life. There is no excellent beauty, that hath not some strangeness in the proportion. A man cannot tell whether

美德，犹如宝石，镶嵌朴素为最佳，因此，一个人即便没有精致面容，但清秀外表加上美德便已足矣。仪表端庄，胜过面容姣美。

非众之所见，绝美之人通常都德行不佳。似乎其天性只忙于追求不犯错误，而不是培养美德。因此，他们看似学识渊博，其实缺乏精神修养；他们所学，只是行为，而非德行。但也非全都如此：奥古斯都·凯撒、提图斯·维斯帕西亚努斯、法王菲利普、英王爱德华四世、雅典的亚西比德、波斯帝王伊斯梅尔，他们都是有着崇高精神修养之人，而且也是当时最为貌美之人。仪表端正之美胜于颜色之美；而谦和得体又胜于仪表端正。美之绝佳部分，非图画所能表达，非一眼所能识穿。所有极致之美，在其比例配合上都有其奇异之处。无人能够道出阿佩利斯和艾伯特·杜勒谁人更胜一筹，他俩绘制人像，其一擅长利用几何比例，其一擅长采集众人脸型之最优之处，以成绝美之人像。

我认为，画家如此作出的人像，除了取悦自己，恐无法讨他人欢心。

Apelles, or Albert Durer, were the more trifler; whereof the one, would make a personage by geo-metrical proportions; the other, by taking the best parts out of divers faces, to make one excellent.

Such personages, I think, would please nobody, but the painter that made them. Not but I think a painter may make a better face than ever was; but he must do it by a kind of felicity (as a musician that maketh an excellent air in music), and not by rule. A man shall see faces, that if you examine them part by part, you shall find never a good; and yet altogether do well. If it be true that the principal part of beauty is in decent motion, cer-tainly it is no marvel, though persons in years seem many times more amiable; pulchrorum autumnus pulcher; for no youth can be comely but by pardon, and considering the youth, as to make up the comeliness. Beauty is as summer fruits, which are easy to corrupt, and cannot last; and for the most part it makes a dissolute youth, and an age a little out of countenance; but yet cer-tainly again, if it light well, it maketh virtue shine, and vices blush.

我承认，画家确实可以绘制出比以往更为漂亮的脸庞，但是想要做到这一点，他并不能循规蹈矩，而必须不拘一格（就像能够利用音乐创造出绝妙氛围的音乐家）。世人必定见过这样的面孔，如若逐个观察每一部位，你会发现全无美感，但是整体观之，则和谐美观。如果美之主体在于举止优雅得体，那么说年长之人会更加温和可亲、美人迟暮而更美，便不足为怪了。恕我直言，少年之俊美是因其年轻朝气补其形态之不足。貌美有如夏日果实，易腐而不易保存。而世上大多数美人，年少时言行放荡，年长后则面露惭色。但仍是开篇那句，如若镶嵌得当，貌美会使善行大放异彩，让恶习羞愧难当。

Learning to Love Yourself
学会爱自己

© Leslie Karen Lobell

According to the song written by Michael Masser and Linda Creed, Greatest Love of All, "The greatest love of all / Is easy to achieve / Learning to love yourself / It is the greatest love of all." I agree that, for many people, self-love may be the greatest and most important love they ever experience in this lifetime. However, for so many people, "learning to love yourself" does not seem so "easy to achieve". For most of us, genuine self-love seems so elusive, so much harder to grasp than we expected. Now, I would like to give some practical suggestions—some first steps—on how to learn to love yourself.

I have made the **analogy**[①] that, if you keep giving to others without giving to yourself, it is like pouring water from a vessel. If you pour and pour without ever refilling it, eventually, it will run dry. So, if we are like that

① analogy [ə'næləd͡ʒi] n. 类比；相似，类似

迈克尔·马瑟和琳达·柯丽德写的歌曲《最伟大的爱》有这样的歌词，“最伟大的爱 / 很容易实现 / 学会爱自己 / 它是最伟大的爱。”我认同这句歌词，因为对许多人来说，自爱可能是他们终其一生所能体验到的最伟大、最重要的爱。然而，对于很多人来说，“学会爱自己”似乎也不那么“容易实现”。至于我们大多数人，真正的自爱似乎如此难以捉摸，比我们想象的更难掌握。现在，我想给出一些实用的建议——几个最简单的步骤——关于如何学会爱自己。

我用自爱打个比方。如果你持续给予他人关爱而没有关爱自己，就像是从一个容器往外倒水：如果你一直往外倒，却始终没有往里面加水，最终它将会干涸。所以，如果我们就是那样的容器，我们应该如何为自己充电、补充能量，不断地充实自己，让我们有力量和爱去给予他人和这个世界？答案就是：首先关爱自己，把爱给自己。那么，怎样开始呢？

关爱和照顾自己的方式有很多……其可能性是无限的。学习爱自己

vessel, how do we refill, recharge, re-energize, and replenish ourselves, so that we will have energy and love to give to others and to the world? The answer is: by loving and giving to ourselves, first. How do we begin to do this?

There are many ways for us to love and to care for ourselves...The possibilities are infinite. One way to learn to love yourself is to act as if you already do (i.e., "Fake it till you make it"). An important way to love yourself is to **nourish**[①] and care for your body: eat healthy foods and exercise regularly. You may want to "treat" yourself to things like a massage, a facial, a pedicure, or a gym membership. Taking breaks and having fun are important, as well. Whether alone, with a friend, or with a partner, you may want to have a night out on the town: go out for a nice dinner, go dancing, and/or attend the theater, a concert, the ballet, or a movie. If you tend to be a workaholic—or if you are more a saver than a spender—then perhaps it is time to take a well-deserved, long-overdue vacation. Of course, treating yourself does not need to involve great expense: you can take a bubble bath, eat dinner at home by candlelight, take a walk on the beach, swim in the ocean (those waters are very healing), or watch a sunset. Perhaps you enjoy taking time to paint or to write. These are just a few ideas. You can put your own imagination to work.

Another way to enhance self-love and self-esteem is to be aware of your self-talk (those things that you say to yourself inside your head). Speak to yourself in ways that are more kind, and less mean or abusive. Many of us have very harsh inner critics: When we make a mistake, this critical voice

① nourish [ˈnʌriʃ] v. 滋养，给营养；培育；怀有

的方法之一就是想象你已经达到某个目标，然后去采取行动（如“假装做到直到你真正做到”）。爱自己的另一个重要方法是关注和呵护你的身体：吃健康的食物，定期锻炼。你可以让自己享受一次按摩，做一次面部或脚部护理，或者加入健身俱乐部。注意多加休息、享受生活乐趣也是很重要的。无论是孤身一人，还是与朋友或伴侣一起，你可以在晚上外出去城里：出去吃一顿大餐，跳跳舞，去剧院看看话剧，听听音乐会，观赏芭蕾舞，又或者看场电影。如果你想做一个工作狂——或者你更像是一个储蓄者而不是一个挥金如土的人，那么也许是时候去当之无愧地度过一个姗姗来迟的假期。当然，善待自己并不一定需要花费巨大的代价：你可以洗一个泡泡浴，在家里吃顿烛光晚餐，在海滩上散散步，到海里去游游泳（海水的疗养效果非常好），或看看日落。也许你喜欢花点时间去画画或写点东西。以上列举的只是几个想法而已，你可以充分发挥自己的想象力。

另一种提高自尊自爱的方式，就是要了解你的自我对话（你在脑袋里对自己说的话）。对自己说话的方式，应该更和善，避免刻薄和咒骂。我们许多人会在内心很严厉地批评自己：当我们犯了错时，脑子里

inside our head beats up on us, saying things like, "That was so stupid!...I can't do anything right!...What a loser!" We need to replace these negative messages with other, more positive ones. For example, "I made a mistake. That's okay: That is how I learn. I'll know better the next time." With awareness, over time, you can "catch yourself" when your self-talk is negative, and change the message to something more positive and "ego-enhancing".

Don't just "catch yourself being wrong". "Catch yourself being right". In other words, don't just catch the voice of your inner critic, and stop it from beating up on you. When you do something well, or when you find yourself saying the right things to yourself or to others, be sure to reward yourself: acknowledge yourself verbally, give yourself a pat on the back, or treat yourself to something special.

Yet another way you can learn to love yourself is by being in the practice of using positive affirmations. Take some time to come up with the qualities that you most want to embody. Choose about two or three to focus on for any one period of time. Then try this for at least a month: Repeat those qualities daily, telling yourself that you are those things, already. Whether or not you currently believe it, say it anyway...Again, "Fake it till you make it." For example, take time to tell yourself, each day, "I am happy and successful" or "I am beautiful and bright" or "I love my body: I feel healthy and in balance" or "I am loving, caring, and worthy of love" or "I am powerful and self-confident"...whatever qualities you wish to be. You may want to write out these affirmations and post them someplace where you will see them

批评的声音就会把我们自己痛批一顿，说类似这样的话："那真是太蠢了！……我什么事也做不好！……我真是一个失败者！"我们需要用更正面、积极的信息替代这些负面信息。例如，"我犯了一个错误。没关系，就当付了学费。下次我就会做得更好。"你有意识地这样做，久而久之，随着时间的推移，当你对自己诉说负面信息的时候，你就可以"抓住自己"，改说一些更积极的、"自我提升"的话。

不要总是"发现自己是错误的"，你应该也"发现自己是正确的"。换句话说，不要只是听到你内心批评的声音，不要被它打败。当你做得不错时，或者当你发现对自己或他人说正确的事情时，要奖励自己：口头上称赞自己，拍拍自己的肩膀，或者让自己享受一些特别的东西。

另一种学会爱自己的方法是在实践中使用正面的肯定。花些时间想出你最想体现的品质，然后在一段时间内选择关注两或三个品质。尝试坚持至少一个月：每天重复那些品质，告诉自己，你已经拥有这些品质。无论你目前是否相信它，请对自己说……还是那句老话，"假装做到直到你真正做到"。例如，每天花点时间告诉自己："我很快乐、很成功"，"我很漂亮、很聪明"，"我爱我的身体：我很健康、很平衡"，"我很有爱心，总是关怀他人，值得被爱"，或"我很强大、很自信"……任何你想要的品质。你可以把这些正面肯定写下来，粘贴在你经常看到的地方：浴室的镜子上，冰箱门上，卧室的时钟边，电脑显示器上方，或办

regularly: on the bathroom mirror, on the refrigerator door, by the clock in your bedroom, atop your computer monitor, or somewhere in front of your desk at work. Even if, at first, you feel silly or uncomfortable repeating or reading these phrases, you may find that you grow into and become these qualities. You may even realize that you embodied them all along; you just had not realized it.

So, go ahead. Love yourself. Be good to yourself. Treat yourself well. Replenish yourself. You will discover that, the more you love yourself, the more you will be able to give love to others—and the more others will want to be around you and give back to you. This is a win-win situation. Loving yourself will **ultimately**[①] benefit the lives of others you encounter, as well as your own life.

① ultimately ['ʌltimitli] adv. 最后；最终

公桌前的某个位置。即使起初你觉得重复阅读这些短语很傻或不舒服，但你可能会发现自己正在成长，并逐渐具备这些品质。你甚至可能意识到你身上其实一直都有这些品质，只是之前你没发现而已。

所以，去吧，去爱你自己。善待自己，照顾自己，充实自己。你会发现，你给自己的爱愈多，你能够给予他人的爱也愈多，他人也会越想陪伴你左右，把爱回馈给你。这是一个双赢的过程。爱自己最终会有利于你所遇到的他人的生活以及你自己的生活。

I Will Laugh at the World
我要笑遍全世界

◎ Og Mandino

No living creature can laugh except man. Trees may bleed when they are wounded, and beasts in the field will cry in pain and hunger, yet only I have the gift of laughter and it is mine to use whenever I choose. Henceforth I will cultivate the habit of laughter.

I will smile and my digestion will improve; I will chuckle and my burdens will be lightened; I will laugh and my life will be lengthened for this is the great secret of long life and now it is mine.

I will laugh at the world.

And most of all, I will laugh at myself for man is most **comical**① when he takes himself too seriously. Never will I fall into this trap of the mind. For though I be nature's greatest miracle am I not still a mere grain tossed about by the winds of time? Do I truly know whence I came or whither I am bound? Will my concern for this day not seem foolish ten years hence? Why should I permit the petty happenings of today to disturb me? What can take place

① comical ['kɒmɪk(ə)l] adj. 滑稽的，好笑的

作者简介

奥格·曼狄诺（Og Mandino，1924—1996），美国杰出企业家、作家和演讲家。他是当今世界上最能激发读者阅读热情和自学精神的作家，也是最受追捧的演讲家之一。他的 18 部作品被译成 18 种语言，销量超过 3000 万册。代表作《世界上最伟大的推销员》等。

笑是人特有的功能。树木遭到砍伐会悲痛，草原上的野兽会因疼痛和饥饿而哀哭，但唯有我有这样的恩赐——我可以大笑，而且随时都可以。那么，我要养成大笑的习惯。

我要微笑，因为它能促进消化；我要轻笑，因为它能减轻压力；我要大笑，因为它能增加寿命。大笑是长寿最大的秘密，现在，我已拥有了大笑的习惯。

我要笑遍全世界。

首先，我要向自己大笑，因为人太严肃紧张时是最滑稽可笑的。我永远都不会犯这样愚蠢的错误。尽管我知道自己是自然界最伟大的奇迹，但我还只是一颗小小的尘埃，被时间的大风吹来吹去，肆意摆弄，难道不是吗？我真的知道我从何处来，要去往何处吗？我对今天如此重视，在十年后会不会看起来很可笑？为什么我允许这些琐碎的小事来烦扰自

before this sun sets which will not seem insignificant in the river of centuries?

And how can I laugh when confronted with man or deed which offends me so as to bring forth my tears or my curses? Four words I will train myself to say until they become a habit so strong that immediately they will appear in my mind whenever good humor threatens to depart from me. These words, passed down from the ancients, will carry me through every **adversity**① and maintain my life in balance. These four words are: This too shall pass.

For all worldly things shall indeed pass. When I am heavy with heartache I shall **console**② myself that this too shall pass; when I am puffed with success I shall warn myself that this too shall pass. When I am strangled in poverty I shall tell myself that this too shall pass; when I am burdened with wealth I shall tell myself that this too shall pass. Yea, verily, where is he who built the pyramid? Is he not buried within its stone? And will the pyramid, one day, not also be buried under sand? If all things shall pass why should I be of concern for today?

I will laugh at the world.

I will paint this day with laughter; I will frame this night in song. Never will I labor to be happy; rather will I remain too busy to be sad. I will enjoy today's happiness today. It is not grain to be stored in a box. It is not wine to be saved in a jar. It cannot be saved for tomorrow. It must be sown and reaped on the same day and this I will do, henceforth.

---

① adversity [əd'vɜːsɪtɪ] n. 逆境；不幸；灾难；灾祸

② console [kən'səʊl] v. 安慰；慰藉

己？在历史的漫漫长河中，不寻常的日落前会有什么样的记忆？

当我碰到令我不快的人或事时，我会流泪、咒骂，此时，我还能笑得出来吗？但我会训练自己记住一句话，直到它们成为一种条件反射，我一恼怒伤心时，它们就会出现在我的脑海里。这句话是从远古时代流传下来的，而且一直存留在我的脑海中，它会帮助我应对一切逆境。它就是：一切都会过去。

所有尘事都如过眼云烟。当我疼痛难耐时，我会安慰自己，一切都会过去；当我因一点成功而洋洋得意时，我会提醒自己，一切都会过去；当我身无分文时，我会告诉自己，一切都会过去；当我为钱财所累时，我会告诉自己，一切都会过去。那个造金字塔的人，他现在在哪儿？难道他现在不躺在用石头堆积起来的坟墓里吗？还有金字塔，难道不会有那么一天，连它也要埋在沙土中吗？如果一切都会过去，我为什么要为眼前的事锱铢必较呢？

我要笑遍全世界。

我要用笑声描绘白天，用歌声装饰夜晚。我不会苦苦地追寻幸福，而要在繁忙中忘记悲伤。我要享受今天的幸福。它不是箱子里搜集起来的粮食，也不是酒桶里储存起来的酒；它不能存留到明天，在同一天就要播种和收割。从此，我也要这样播种和收割幸福。

在我的大笑中，所有事情都会回到它原来的样子。我会对失败大笑，

And with my laughter all things will be reduced to their proper size. I will laugh at my failures and they will vanish in clouds of new dreams; I will laugh at my successes and they will shrink to their true value. I will laugh at evil and it will die untasted; I will laugh at goodness and it will thrive and abound.

Henceforth will I shed only tears of sweat, for those of sadness or remorse or **frustration**① are of no value in the market place whilst each smile can be exchanged for gold and each kind word, spoken from my heart, can build a castle.

Never will I allow myself to become so important, so wise, so dignified, so powerful, that I forget how to laugh at myself and my world. In this matter I will always remain as a child, for only as a child am I given the ability to look up to others; and so long as I look up to another I will never grow too long for my cot.

And so long as I can laugh never will I be poor. This, then, is one of nature's greatest gifts, and I will waste it no more. Only with laughter and happiness can I truly become a success. Only with laughter and happiness can I enjoy the fruits of my labor. Were it not so, far better would it be to fail, for happiness is the wine that sharpens the taste of the meal. To enjoy success I must have happiness, and laughter will be the maiden who serves me.

I will be happy.

I will be successful.

---

① frustration [frʌ'streɪʃn] n. 挫折

它们就会在新梦想的云层中消失殆尽。我会对成功大笑，它们就会收缩，显出真实的价值。我会对邪恶大笑，它们就会灭亡。我会对美好大笑，它们就会越来越兴盛繁荣。

我只会流一种泪水，那就是甜蜜的眼泪。因为无论是悲伤、后悔还是沮丧，都没有任何价值；而每一个微笑都像是金子，我发自内心的每句良言都将造成一座宫殿。

我不会让自己拥有太多的地位、智慧、威望和权力，这样我会忘了如何对自己以及世界大笑。所以，我会一直保持小孩的方式。只有这样，我才能尊重别人，只有尊重别人，我才不会骄傲自大。

只要我还能笑，我就永不贫乏。笑是大自然赋予我最珍贵的礼物之一，我不会浪费丝毫。唯有拥有大笑和快乐，我才能真正地赢得成功。唯有拥有大笑和快乐，我才能得以享受劳动带来的果实。如果没有大笑和快乐，我会一败涂地，因为快乐是增添美食滋味的美酒。要享受成功，我必须要快乐，而大笑就是陪伴我的少女。

我会幸福。

我会成功。

生命不在于完成

Time is a versatile performer. It flies, marches on, heals all wounds, runs out and will tell.

—Franklin P. Jones

时间是个多才多艺的表演者。它能展翅飞翔，能阔步前进，能治愈创伤，能消逝而去，也能揭示真相。

——富兰克林·P. 琼斯

If I Rest, I Rust

我若停下，便会腐朽

◎ Orison Marden

The significant inscription found on an old key—"If I rest, I rust"—would be an excellent motto for those who are afflicted with the slightest bit of idleness. Even the most industrious person might adopt it with advantage to serve as a reminder that, if one allows his faculties to rest, like the iron in the unused key, they will soon show signs of rust and, ultimately, cannot do the work required of them.

Those who would attain the heights reached and kept by great men must keep their faculties polished by constant use, so that they may unlock the doors of knowledge, the gate that guard the entrances to the professions, to science, art, literature, agriculture—every department of human endeavor.

Industry keeps bright the key that opens the treasury of achievement. If Hugh Miller, after toiling all day in a quarry, had devoted his evenings to rest and recreation, he would never have become a famous geologist. The celebrated mathematician, Edmund Stone, would never have published a

作者简介

奥里森·马登（Orison Marden，1848—1942），被公认为美国成功学的奠基人和最伟大的成功励志导师，成功学之父。《成功》杂志创始人，著有大量成功学著作，代表作《一生的资本》《思考与成功》《伟大的励志书》《成功学原理》等。

一把旧钥匙上铭刻着一段极有意义的话——“我若停下，便会腐朽”——这对那些慵懒之人来说可谓是一句至理名言。就连最勤劳的人也可用这句话作为时刻提醒自己的警钟。如果一个人纵容自己停下了脚步，就如一把废弃钥匙上的铁，很快就会滋生斑斑锈迹，最终再也无法完成使命。

只有那些能在学术上不断坚持这一信念的人，才能得以达到一种伟人的高度。这样才能让他们开启知识的大门，进入科学、艺术、文学、农业——每一个促使人类进步的重要领域。

勤勉能使这把开启成就宝箱的钥匙持续光亮。如果休·米勒在采石场工作一天后，把晚上的时间用来休息消遣，他也就不会成为名垂青史的地质学家。如果把闲暇时刻慵懒度过，著名数学家爱德蒙·斯通也永远出版不了数学词典，永远不会发现数学的精髓所在；如果苏格兰青年

mathematical dictionary, never have found the key to science of mathematics, if he had given his spare moments to idleness, had the little Scotch lad, Ferguson, allowed the busy brain to go to sleep while he tended sheep on the hillside instead of calculating the position of the stars by a string of beads, he would never have become a famous astronomer.

Labor vanquishes all—not inconstant, spasmodic, or ill-directed labor; but faithful, unremitting, daily effort toward a well-directed purpose. Just as truly as eternal vigilance is the price of liberty, so is eternal industry the price of noble and enduring success.

弗格森在放羊的山坡上无所事事，让忙碌的大脑进入睡眠状态，而不是通过珠式星象计算星星的位置，他也永远成不了一位著名的天文学家。

劳动能够征服一切——不是那种三天打鱼两天晒网的劳动，也不是走错方向的劳动，而是有信念的、坚持不懈的、日复一日朝着正确方向走去的付出。正如保持高度的警惕是自由的代价，坚持勤勉也是走向崇高和成功的必经之路。

The Meaning of Your Life
生命的意义

◎ Ineke Van Lint

Your dream is the reason for the way you are. Your dream is not a **coincidence**①[①]. Your dream is who you are. You should pursue it! Your dream gives you a sense of meaning and purpose, and drives you on into your chosen future. Your dream is the meaning of your life!

Everybody has goals and dreams. These dreams are at the center of who you really are. It is the core **essence**[②] of who you are as a person, and the very purpose of your being. What you are dreaming of accomplishing in your life is God's way of getting you involved in his Master Plan.

You were gifted with a set of dreams and talents, in the hope that you would act out these passions, follow your dreams and thusly move forward in life. It's really a great pity that we've been told already since early childhood that we should stop dreaming and start "living". What a mistake! Living is

① coincidence [ko'ɪnsɪdəns] n. 巧合；一致性；同时发生

② essence ['ɛsəns] n. 本质，实质；精华；香精

你的梦想是你存在的理由。你的梦想不是一种巧合。你的梦想证明了你是谁。你应该追寻梦想！梦想给予你意义和目标，驱使你投入到你所选择的未来当中。梦想是你生命的意义！

每个人都有目标和梦想。那些梦想是你真实自我的中心。那是你作为一个人，真实自我的核心本质，是你存在的真正目的。你梦想在你人生中所实现的成就，就是上帝带你进入他的“大师计划”的方式。

你被赋予拥有梦想和天赋的能力，希望你能把这些激情表现出来，追随梦想而去，在生命中向前发展。但是，确实遗憾的是，我们从小就被教育要停止做梦，开始“生活”。这是个多大的错误啊！生活就是梦想！这就是为什么我们会在这儿：追寻我们的梦想！不是出于自私的原因，是为了每个人自身的利益。

通过追寻我的梦想，我逐渐成为一个更好的人，一个快乐的人，我

dreaming! This is exactly why we are here: to pursue our dreams! Not for selfish reasons, but for the sake of everybody.

By following my dreams, I am becoming a better person, a happy person, shining brightly like a sun, lightening up the lives of those around me. If I decide to forget about my dreams, then I will become like a plant without water or sunlight, leaves hanging down, begging for water and looking rather **miserable**①. Am I of any help to myself or to the world when I abandon my dreams?

Why then does it seem to be so difficult to follow your dream? First, because of the anti-dream-program running in your head, a program installed when you were just a kid. Second, because your dream is always outside of your comfort zone. Pursuing your dream requires conscious effort, growth and change; this can feel somewhat uncomfortable in the beginning. You may experience some fears and worries, but this is normal. Don't focus on the fear, but focus on the dream. This way the dream becomes more important to you than the fear. Spending your life in fear and worry surely isn't part of the Master Plan. Ask yourself this question: "What do I really want? Realizing my dreams, or getting stuck in my fears? Do I choose to follow my dream and harvest satisfaction, freedom, happiness and abundance? Or do I lock myself up in my room with my good old irritation, lack of energy, fear, fatigue and depression?" The choice is yours. As long as your dreams appeal more to you than your fears, you will find the energy and courage to move on.

---

① miserable ['mɪzərəbəl] adj. 悲惨的；痛苦的；卑鄙的

像太阳般散发光芒，照亮我身边的人的生活。如果我决定忘记自己的梦想，那么我就会像没有水分和阳光的植物一样，叶子枯零凋落，祈求水的滋润，看起来相当悲惨。在我抛弃梦想的时候，我对自己或世界来说有任何益处吗?

为什么追寻梦想看起来如此困难? 第一，因为在你脑中有抵制梦想的程序，这种程序在你小时候就被安装了。第二，因为你的梦想总是在你的舒适带范围之外。追寻梦想需要你自觉地努力、成长和改变。在开始，这会让你感到有点不舒适。你也许经历过一些恐惧和担忧，但这很正常。不要只关注恐惧，而要关注梦想。这样，梦想就会比恐惧变得更加重要。显然，将你的光阴都花在恐惧和担忧上可不是“大师计划”的一部分。扪心自问：“我到底想要什么? 实现自己的梦想还是陷入恐惧之中? 我是该选择追随梦想、收获满足、自由、幸福和丰富人生呢? 还是我要把自己锁在房间里，过着自己原来的生活，远离能量、恐惧、疲劳和沮丧? ”这都是你的选择。只要你的梦想比恐惧对你更有吸引力，你就会找到能量和勇气继续前行。

你的梦想是由你决定的，你必须做些事来成就自己。请用你的整个生命付诸实践，表达你对“大师计划”的信念。大声说：“我不知道我如何能做到，但是只要我相信这点并追随自己的梦想，那么世界就会一

Your dream is your calling, something you have to do to fulfill you. Commit yourself to it with your entire being. Express your faith in the Master Plan. Say, "I don't know how I will do it, but if I just believe in it and follow my dream, then the Universe will show me, step by step, how to proceed." Have faith, take action, and then watch what happens. Your dream is linked to your mission here on earth, your unique calling in life. The seeds of your dream have been sown in your heart and mind, and it is your job to help them grow, to develop your talents. Usually your dream will involve being of service to others to make their lives easier, better, more joyful and more beautiful. What is your contribution to other's lives? Exactly how do you make their lives better? What do you add to them? Is it beauty, joy, enthusiasm, faith, music, art, paintings, fragrance, motivation, a smile, some hope, self-esteem? Choose to follow your dream. It is your responsibility. You must do it. It's part of God's Plan. This is His way of helping this planet uplift its energy. Isn't it wonderful?

By following your dream, not only do you please yourself, but you are also uplifting the whole of humanity! If you ignore your dreams, do you realize how many people will be affected? It is God's Plan and therefore it can never be selfish. The more you pursue your dreams, the more exciting your life becomes! God is going to use you in ways you never imagined possible. And the only side effect is: feeling good! Get your dreams off the shelf! Put your goals in front of you, and follow them. Focus. Strive. This IS what you should be doing, this IS what you are here for!

步步地告诉我该如何进行。”永存信念，采取行动，然后细心观察发生的事。你的梦想和你在地球上的使命是连在一起的，这是你生命中的独特之处。梦想的种子已播种在你的心田和脑海，你的职责就是帮助它们成长，去发展你的才能。梦想通常包括为别人提供服务，让他们的生活更容易、更舒适、更欢乐、更美好。你对别人生活的贡献又是什么呢?你又是怎样让别人的生活更美好的呢?你为他们提供了什么?是美丽、快乐、热情、信念、音乐、艺术、绘画、芳香、动机、微笑、希望还是自尊?选择追随你的梦想吧。这是你的责任，你必须要做。这是上帝计划中的一部分。这是上帝帮助他的世界提升能量的方式。这难道不奇妙吗?

追随你的梦想，不只是让自我满足，同时你还升华了整个人性！如果你忽视梦想，你意识到会有多少人受你影响吗?这是上帝的计划，所以它永不会自私。你越追随自己的梦想，你的生活就会越刺激！上帝将会以你从未想过的方式发挥你的才能。然而，唯一的副作用就是：感觉良好！拾起你现在的梦想，把目标摆在你的面前，然后追随它们。全神贯注、奋斗拼搏，这就是你现在应该做的，这也就是你存在的原因！

你的存在是为了梦想，是为了实现梦想。实现它们，快乐生活！这就是事情的意义。现在是时候回到原本了。你生活的本质是你的梦想！

You are here to dream, and to live your dreams! Live them out and live it up! This is how things were meant to be. It's time to get back to basics. The essence of your life is your dream! What have you always been dreaming about, ever since you were a kid? Visualize it, define it, and then go for it! Become happy and share that happiness with the world. My dream in sharing these articles is to help others discover their reason of being here on earth, to help you discover your own unique talents , to help you realize your potential and to help you manifest your personal dreams.

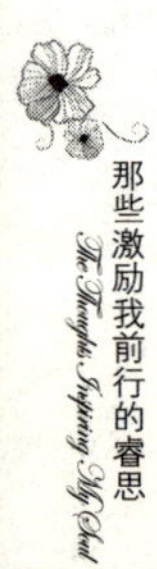

从你小时候起，你一直梦想的是什么？把它形象化，明确下来，然后追寻它！快乐地生活并和世界分享你的快乐。我的梦想就是通过分享这些文章，帮助别人发现他们存在于地球的理由，去帮助你发现你自己独特的才能，去帮助你发挥自己的潜能，并实现你的个人梦想。

Roll Away the Stones

推开石头

◎ Pearl S. Buck

I enjoy life because I am endlessly interested in people and their growth. My interest leads me to widen my knowledge of people, and this in turn compels me to believe in the common goodness of mankind. I believe that the normal human heart is born good. That is, it's born sensitive and feeling, eager to be approved and to approve, hungry for simple happiness and the chance to live. It neither wishes to be killed, nor to kill. If through circumstances, it is overcome by evil, it never becomes entirely evil. There remain in it elements of good, however recessive, which continue to hold the possibility of restoration.

I believe in human beings, but my faith is without sentimentality. I know that in environments of uncertainty, fear, and hunger, the human being is dwarfed and shaped without his being aware of it, just as the plant struggling under a stone does not know its own condition. Only when the stone is removed can it spring up freely into the light. But the power to spring up is inherent, and only death puts an end to it. I feel no need for any other faith

作者简介

赛珍珠（Pearl S. Buck，1892—1973），美国著名女作家，是唯一同时获得普利策奖和诺贝尔奖的女作家，也是作品流传语种最多的美国作家。出生之后不久随传教士父母来到中国，先后生活和工作于淮安、镇江、苏州、南京和庐山等地，共近40年。代表作《大地》。

我热衷于生活，因为我向来对人类及其发展充满了兴趣，也正是这一兴致促使我不断拓宽对人类知识的了解。这反而使我坚信，人类共有某些向善的普遍性。我相信人大都生而善良。也就是说，人天生敏感多情，希望被认同也愿意认同他人，渴求简单的幸福和生存下去的机会。人不希望被杀害，也不希望去杀害别人。即使偶有邪念，其心智也不会被完全控制。因此人心都是肉做的，善良的一面无论怎样退隐于内心深处，也总有可能恢复到善良至上的本性。

我相信人类，但我绝非感情用事之人。我知道，在无把握的未来、时常的恐惧、饥寒交迫的环境中，人类便不能意识到他们的发展遇到了多大的阻力，就如石缝下面的植物努力生长，却不知自己的困境是被石头压迫着的。唯有推开石头，想办法摆脱困境，植物才能生机勃发、沐浴阳光。然而，植物与生具有自然生长的力量，这是一种恐怕只有死亡才能将其终止的力量。由此，我愈发觉得在关于人类信念的分析上，

than my faith in human beings.

Like Confucius of old, I am absorbed in the wonder of earth, and the life upon it, and I cannot think of heaven and the angels. I have enough for this life. If there is no other life, then this one has been enough to make it worth being born, myself a human being. With so profound a faith in the human heart and its power to grow toward the light, I find here reason and cause enough for hope and confidence in the future of mankind. The common sense of people will surely prove to them someday that mutual support and cooperation are only sensible for the security and happiness of all. Such faith keeps me continually ready and purposeful with energy to do what one person can towards shaping the environment in which the human being can grow with freedom. This environment, I believe, is based upon the necessity for security and friendship.

I take heart in a promising fact that the world contains food supplies sufficient for the entire earth population. Our knowledge of medical science is already sufficient to improve the health of the whole human race. Our resources and education, if administered on a world scale, can lift the intelligence of the race. All that remains is to discover how to administer upon a world scale, the benefits which some of us already have. In other words, to return to my simile, the stone must be rolled away. This too can be done, as a sufficient number of human beings come to have faith in themselves and in each other. Not all will have such faith at the same moment, but there is a growing number who have the faith.

自己的见解比其他见解都深刻许多。

就如孔夫子一般，我也深深沉浸在地球仙境和美好的生活中，让我不用再去渴望置身天堂或者变为天使的愿景。就这样去感悟人生，足矣。如果没有来世，今世也不枉我来走一趟，成为一个真正的人。带着这种人心之善以及向往光明的坚定信念，使我对人类的未来也充满希望和信心。人类的常识一定会在未来的某一天向他们证明，互相支持与合作只会对全人类的安全和幸福带来实质上的帮助。这种信念让我保持充沛的精力，带着最明确的目的，乐此不疲地，为营造能让人类自由发展的环境略尽绵力。而我相信，安全保障和与人为善是营造这个环境的必要前提。

我鼓足勇气来面对这个充满光明前景的未来：世界丰富的物产供养着人类；我们的医药科学大大改善了人类的健康状况；我们的各种资源和教育水平，若放在世界范围内进行统一管理，便能提高整个人类的智力；剩下要做的，便是找到一个办法，去统一管理世界上一些蓬勃发展的有益之事，其中有些事情我们已经在做了。换言之，回到我刚才的比喻，也就是说必须推开石头这一点。这也是能做到的，因为我们有相当多的人已逐渐树立了对自己和他人的信念，彼此也相互信任。虽然并不是所有的人在同一时刻都具备这种信念，但可喜的是，找到自己信念的人数已在不断增加。

半个世纪以前，没人考虑一些重大问题：世界食物短缺、人类健康

Half a century ago, no one had thought of world food, world health, world education. Many are thinking today of these things. In the midst of possible world war, of wholesale destruction, I find my only question this: are there enough people now who believe? Is there time enough left for the wise to act? It is a contest between ignorance and death, or wisdom and life. My faith in humanity stands firm.

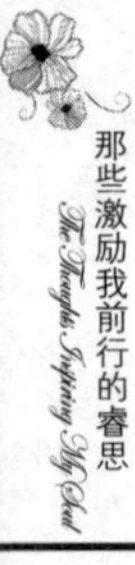

状况低下、教育资源匮乏。而今天就有许多人考虑去改善这些状况了。在可能会发生的世界战争中，在大规模的毁灭过程中，我唯一的疑惑是：有足够多的人树立自己的信仰了吗？有足够的时间让智者采取行动吗？这是无知与死亡之间，或是智慧与生命之间的竞赛。我对人类的信念坚定不移。

"To Be or Not to Be"

生存亦或毁灭

◎ William Lyon Phelps

"To be or not to be". Outside the Bible, these six words are the most famous in all the literature of the world. They were spoken by Hamlet when he was thinking aloud, and they are the most famous words in Shakespeare because Hamlet was speaking not only for himself but also for every thinking man and woman. To be or not to be—to live or not to live, to live richly and abundantly and eagerly, or to live dully and meanly and scarcely. A philosopher once wanted to know whether he was alive or not, which is a good question for everyone to put to himself occasionally. He answered it by saying, "I think, therefore I am."

But the best definition of existence I ever saw was one given by another philosopher who said, "To be is to be in relations." If this is true, then the more relations a living thing has, the more it is alive. To live abundantly means simply to increase the range and intensity of our relations. Unfortunately we are so constituted that we get to love our routine. But apart from our

作者简介

威廉·里昂·费尔浦斯（William Lyon Phelps，1865—1943），美国耶鲁大学教授，世界知名学者，以博学与智慧闻名于世，著有《现代小说家评论集》《20世纪戏剧》等小说理论研究书籍。

除了《圣经》之外，“生存亦或毁灭”或许是世界文学史上最著名的六个字了。哈姆雷特偶然自说自话地道出了这个真理，而这六个字也就成了莎士比亚作品中的经典，因为哈姆雷特不只是说的他自己，也代表了这个世界上每一个疑惑思考的人们。生存亦或毁灭——是否要生存得有价值，是否要生活得丰富多彩，充满希望，还是只活得索然无味，枯燥无趣。一位哲学家曾试图弄明白自己是否还活着，这个问题也适用于我们每个人不时问问自己。对此这位哲学家的回答是：“我思故我在。”

但我所知对生存最好的定义却来自另一位哲学家：“活着即是联系。”如果这话不假，那么一个关联越多的生命就越能证明自己的真实存在。活得充实，简单来说，指的是扩大和加强我们的各种联系。但不幸的是，我们却过于习惯墨守陈规。然而，除开被日常琐事占据的时间，我们真正意义上的生活有多少呢？那么，如果你只是对你的日常琐事感兴趣，那你的生命价值也就局限在了这个圈子里。至于其他方面，如诗歌、散

regular occupation how much are we alive? If you are interested only in your regular occupation, you are alive only to that extent. So far as other things are concerned—poetry and prose, music, pictures, sports, unselfish friendships, politics, international affairs—you are dead.

Contrariwise, it is true that every time you acquire a new interest—even more, a new accomplishment—you increase your power of life. No one who is deeply interested in a large variety of subjects can remain unhappy; the real pessimist is the person who has lost interest.

Bacon said that a man dies as often as he loses a friend. But we gain new life by contacts, new friends. What is supremely true of living objects is no less true of ideas, which are also alive. Where your thoughts are, there will your live be also. If your thoughts are confined only to your business, only to your physical welfare, only to the narrow circle of the town in which you live, then you live in a narrow circumscribed life. But if you are interested in what is going on in China, then you are living in China; if you're interested in the characters of a good novel, then you are living with those highly interesting people; if you listen intently to fine music, you are away from your immediate surroundings and living in a world of passion and imagination.

To be or not to be—to live intensely and richly, or merely to exist, that depends on ourselves. Let's widen and intensify our relations. While we live, let us live!

文、音乐、绘画、体育、无私友谊、政治、国家事务，等等——你只是死人一个。

反之，每当你收获一种新的兴趣——或者说取得了一份新的成就——你就会更加懂得如何去获得真正意义上的生活。一个兴趣广泛的人是可以远离郁闷沮丧的；而真正悲观的人是那些不知兴趣何在的人。

培根说过，失去朋友的人必死无疑。但是，凭着新拓展的人脉联系，我们就能获得全新的生活。这个对活物来说千真万确的道理，一定程度上也完全适用于人的思想，因为思想也是活的。你的思想和你的生命同在。如果你的思想仅限于你的工作范围，仅限于你的物质利益，仅限于你生活的狭隘圈子，那你就只能在这多方局限里终结一生。但如果你对当下的中国时事感兴趣，那你便可说自己活在中国；如果你阅读一本好小说时，思想完全融入于它的文字之中，你便可以算得上活在许多活灵活现的小说角色中间；如果你醉心于美妙的音乐，你就会脱离现实的生活环境，徜徉在一个充满想象与激情的神奇音乐世界之中。

生存还是毁灭——热情丰富地生存下去，还是只简单存在一副生命躯壳，都取决于我们自己。但愿我们能不断扩充和增强自己的种种联系。只要我们还有生命，就要真正地活着。

It's Not About How to Get Things Done: Are You Enjoying Life

生命不在于完成：你享受生活吗

© Amy Twain

We all have our plans in this lifetime but whether we like it or not, time is **apathetic**[1] to our plans. As morbid as it may sound, but we're all going to die someday and we'll be unable to get things done. Then, before we know it, time stops us even before we're ready.

Many tasks left undone, more love, laughter, hugs and smiles to be shared. But alas, we'll never know for how long. The **evanescent**[2], fleeting now is the moment—all that you have and you can enjoy while it lasts. The bygone yesterdays of past is faded into oblivion—memory is all you have.

Then the future remains unknown and a mystery.

But the question is: What are you doing in your life right now—is it even

---

① apathetic [ˌæpəˈθɛtɪk] adj. 冷漠的；无动于衷的，缺乏兴趣的

② evanescent [ˌɛvəˈnɛsənt] adj. 容易消极的；逐渐消失的

我们对于自己的生活都有自己的计划，但是我们是否喜欢这样，貌似时间对我们的计划却无动于衷。这听起来很怪异，但是总有一天我们会死，我们也就不能再完成任务了。那么，在我们明白这点之前，甚至在我们还没准备好时，时间就将我们抛弃了。

我们有很多事情没有完成，比如分享更多的爱、笑声、拥抱和微笑。但是，我们很长时间都不会明白。现在正消逝的就是时间——这也是你所拥有的全部，你只有当它还在的时候才能享受它。离去的昨天被渐渐遗忘，你只剩下了回忆。

然而，未来依旧未知且神秘。

但问题是：在你的人生中，现在你在做什么——这还值得让你花时间和精力吗？你享受这件事吗？它值得你付出精力吗？它有趣并令你满

worth your time and effort? Are you enjoying it? Is it worth your energy? It is fun and fulfilling? Is it giving you the drive—that fire in your belly to keep you alive? Are you motivated with life and keeps you inspired and excited to welcome a new day? Does it give you a chance to change a person's life or contribute something beneficial to **humanity**[1]?

Life is not about how to get things done; it's about how you live the moment. Each precious hour, minute and second of your life that the universe has bestowed you with.

If you think about it, there's a myriad of stuff you'll never get done—and how liberating it feels! It's not upsetting at all. It simply shows you that you don't have to take control of the universe.

It gives you the freedom to be in charge of the work before you, the ones you willingly chosen, which you'll be enjoying the process and not really worrying how to get things done—in the end, makes you enjoy life more.

① humanity [hju'mænɪti] n. 人类；人道；人性

意吗？它给你动力——燃烧你内心的激情，驱使你继续生活吗？你对生活充满积极性吗？你能激情而兴奋地迎接新的一天吗？它有机会让你改变人生或有助于你人性的发展吗？

生命不在于事情是否完成，而在于你怎么活在当下。宇宙已授予你每个珍贵的小时，每一分、每一秒都弥足珍贵。

如果你明白这一点，你就会发现大量你不再想完成的事情——你会感觉到解放的自由！这一点儿也不令人苦恼。这只是表明你不必再控制世界了。

只负责你愿意选择的眼前的工作，这会给你带来自由感。这样，你会享受整个过程，而且不需要担心怎么把事情完成——最终，这会让你更加享受你的生活。

Work, Labor and Play
关于工作、劳作和玩乐

◎ W. H. Auden

So far as I know, Miss Hannah Arendt was the first person to define the essential difference between work and labor. To be happy, a man must feel, firstly, free and, secondly, important. He cannot be really happy if he is compelled by society to do what he does not enjoy doing, or if what he enjoys doing is ignored by society as of no value or importance. In a society where slavery in the strict sense has been abolished, the sign that what a man does is of social value is that he is paid money to do it, but a laborer today can rightly be called a wage slave. A man is a laborer if the job society offers him is of no interest to himself but he is compelled to take it by the necessity of earning a living and supporting his family.

The **antithesis**[①] to labor is play. When we play a game, we enjoy what we are doing, otherwise we should not play it, but it is a purely private activity; society could not care less whether we play it or not.

① antithesis [æn'tɪθɪsɪs] n. 对立面；对照；对仗

作者简介

W.H. 奥登（Wystan Hugh Auden，1907—1973），英国诗人，文学评论家，被认为是继叶芝和艾略特之后英国最重要的诗人。1953 年获得博林根诗歌奖，1956 年获得全国图书奖，1967 年获得全国文学勋章。代表作《短诗结集 1927~1957》《染匠的手》等。

据我所知，汉娜·阿伦特小姐是第一个提出工作和劳作有本质区别的人。一个人如果感到幸福的话，首先他会觉得自由，其次是感到自己的重要性。如果他被社会迫使去做他不喜欢的事，或者他喜欢做的事被社会所忽略，就好像一点也不重要、毫无价值一样，那他就不是真正的幸福。严格意义上说，奴隶制社会已经被废除了，人们所做之事具有社会价值的标志就是别人会付钱给他，但是在今天，劳作者可以被恰当地称为工资奴隶。如果一个人，他对社会提供的工作不感兴趣，但是迫于谋生和养家的需要而被迫接受，那这个人就是个劳作者。

劳作的对立就是玩乐。在我们玩游戏的时候，我们享受我们正在做的事，否则我们是不会玩的，但这是个纯属私人的活动；社会并不关心我们是否要玩乐。

Between labor and play stands work. A man is a worker if he is personally interested in the job which society pays him to do; what from the point of view of society is necessary labor is from his own point of view voluntary play. Whether a job is to be classified as labor or work depends, not on the job itself, but on the tastes of the individual who undertakes it. The difference does not, for example, coincide with the difference between a manual and a mental job; a gardener or a cobbler may be a worker, a bank clerk a laborer. Which a man is can be seen from his attitude toward leisure. To a worker, leisure means simply the hours he needs to relax and rest in order to work efficiently. He is therefore more likely to take too little leisure than too much; workers die of coronaries and forget their wives' birthdays. To the laborer, on the other hand, leisure means freedom from compulsion, so that it is natural for him to imagine that the fewer hours he has to spend laboring, and the more hours he is free to play, the better.

What percentage of the population in a modern technological society are, like myself, in the fortunate position of being workers? At a guess I would say sixteen percent, and I do not think that figure is likely to get bigger in the future.

Technology and the division of labor have done two things: by eliminating in many fields the need for special strength or skill, they have made a very large number of paid occupations which formerly were enjoyable work into boring labor, and by increasing productivity they have reduced the number of necessary laboring hours. It is already possible to imagine a society

在劳作和玩乐之间，还存在着一个概念：工作。如果一个人对于社会付钱让他做的事感兴趣，那他就是个工作者。在社会观念中必需的劳作是工作者眼中自发的玩乐。做事是被归为劳作还是工作，则取决于从事这份工作的人的感觉，而不是这件事本身。譬如，它们之间的区别，与体力劳动和脑力劳动之间的区别是不一样的；园丁或补鞋匠可以是工作者，银行职员也可能是劳作者。确定一个人是劳作者还是工作者，可以从他对休闲的态度来判断。对于工作者来说，休闲仅仅意味他需要放松和休息来更有效率地进行以后的工作。因此，更多地，他的休闲时间远远不够。工作者因为得冠心病而死，他们忘记自己妻子的生日。另一方面，对于劳作者来说，休闲意味着从强迫中解脱并获得自由，所以，自然地，他们会十分希望工作的时间越少，玩乐的时间越多，这样就越好。

在现代科技发展的时代，像我这样幸运的工作者在人口中所占的比例是多少？我推测有 16%，而且我不认为在未来这个数据会变大。

科技的发展和劳动分工有两个影响：通过在很多领域减少对特别力量和技能的需求，它们将大量曾经令人愉悦的有偿劳动变成了枯燥的劳作，随着生产效率的提高，它们减少了必要劳动时间。可以设想这样的一个社会：大多数的人，即劳作者，他们将拥有与早期上层社会所享有

in which the majority of the population, that is to say, its laborers, will have almost as much leisure as in earlier times was enjoyed by the aristocracy. When one recalls how aristocracies in the past actually behaved, the prospect is not cheerful. Indeed, the problem of dealing with boredom may be even more difficult for such a future mass society than it was for **aristocracies**[①]. The latter, for example, ritualized their time; there was a season to shoot grouse, a season to spend in town, etc. The masses are more likely to replace an unchanging ritual by fashion which it will be in the economic interest of certain people to change as often as possible. Again, the masses cannot go in for hunting, for very soon there would be no animals left to hunt. For other aristocratic amusements like gambling, dueling, and warfare, it may be only too easy to find equivalents in dangerous driving, drug-taking, and senseless acts of violence. Workers seldom commit acts of violence, because they can put their aggression into their work, be it physical like the work of a smith, or mental like the work of a scientist or an artist. The role of aggression in mental work is aptly expressed by the phrase "getting one's teeth into a problem."

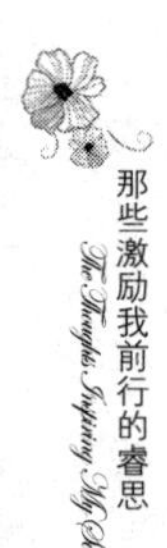

① aristocracy [ˌærɪ'stɑkrəsi] n. 贵族；上层社会

的一样多的休闲时间。当人们回想过去上层社会人们的所作所为时，就可知前景是不乐观的。事实上，比起上层社会，对大众社会来讲，更难解决的是枯燥的问题。譬如，上层社会的人可以使他们的时间程序化；他们分出打猎的季节和在城镇生活的季节等等。而群众更可能的是要尽可能经常通过一些方法，取代一成不变的程式，而这些改变会涉及上层社会的人的经济利益。而且，群众不能出去打猎，因为很快就没有动物留给他们打了。对于上层社会的娱乐消遣，比如赌博、决斗和战争，这些可能很容易在危险驾车、吸毒和愚蠢的暴力行为中找到对等。工作者很少会有暴力行为，因为他们会把自己的侵略性带进他们的工作中，像铁匠从事的体力工作，如科学家或艺术家从事的脑力工作。在脑力劳动中，很好地形容侵略性的作用的一句短语是：“死死咬住某个问题。”

When Ordinary People Achieve Extraordinary Things

凡人造就的非凡事

◎ Jody Williams

I believe it is possible for ordinary people to achieve extraordinary things. For me, the difference between an "ordinary" and an "extraordinary" person is not the title a person might have, but what that person does to make the world a better place for us all.

I don't know why people choose to do what they do. When I was a kid I didn't know what I wanted to be when I grew up, but I knew what I didn't want to do. I didn't want to grow up, have kids, get married. And I certainly didn't think about being an activist. I didn't even really know what one was.

My older brother is deaf. Growing up, I ended up defending him and I often think that is what started me on my path to whatever I am today.

When I was approached with the idea of trying to create a landmine campaign, we were just three people in a small office in Washington, DC in late 1991. I had more than a few ideas about how to begin a campaign, but what if nobody cared? What if nobody responded? But I knew the only way to

作者简介

乔迪·威廉姆斯（Jody Williams），生于1950年，美国著名政治活动家，因其努力禁止杀伤性地雷而为人熟知。她还是人权主义者，尤其看重妇女的权益。1997年，她因为推动国际禁止地雷运动而荣获诺贝尔和平奖。

我一直相信，平凡人也能造就辉煌。在我看来，“平凡人”与“非凡人”之间的区别并不在于当事人有何头衔，而是取决于这个人为改造世界作了多大的贡献。

我不知道人们是怎样选择自己的工作的。小时候，我并不清楚自己长大后应该做什么，但是却对自己不会做的事了如指掌。我不想长大，不想结婚生子。而且我根本不曾考虑过成为一名活动激进分子，我甚至不知道活动家是什么。

我的哥哥是个聋人。长大后，我渐渐地不再处处维护他，还常常想，也许就是这样的变化，造就了今天的我。

1991年末，虽然一共就三个参与者，但在华盛顿区的一个小办公室里，我动了念头想试着开创一个“地雷运动”。对于开创这项活动，我

answer those questions was to accept the challenge.

But if I have any power as an individual, it's because I work with other individuals around the world. We are ordinary people—Jemma from Armenia, Paul from Canada, Kosal from Cambodia, Haboubba from Lebanon, Christian from Norway, Diana from Colombia, Margaret from Uganda and thousands more—who have worked together to bring about extraordinary change. The landmine campaign is not just about landmines—it's about the power of individuals to work with governments in a different way.

I believe in both my right and my responsibility to work to create a world that doesn't glorify violence and war, but where we seek different solutions to our common problems. I believe that these days, daring to voice your opinion, daring to find out information from a variety of sources, can be an act of courage.

I know that holding such beliefs and speaking them publicly is not always easy or comfortable or popular—particularly in the post-9/11 world. But I believe that life isn't a popularity contest. I really don't care what people say about me—and people have said plenty. For me, it's about trying to do the right thing—even when nobody else is looking.

I believe worrying about the problems plaguing our planet without taking steps to confront them is irrelevant. The only thing that changes this world is action.

Most people tend to get caught up in going to college, then getting a job, buying a house and paying the mortgage. Somehow, I've had the desire—and

有许多点子，但如果没人关心怎么办？没人响应怎么办？然而我深知，要知道这些问题的答案，唯有放手一搏进行尝试。

但是，如果我拥有个人的力量，那是因为我与世界上很多有力量的个人共同努力着。我们只是普通人——来自亚美尼亚的杰玛，来自加拿大的保罗，来自柬埔寨的科索，来自黎巴嫩的哈布巴，来自挪威的克里斯汀，来自哥伦比亚的戴安娜，来自乌干达的玛格丽特，以及来自其他各个地方成千上万的人——我们为了创造卓越的变革而通力协作。“地雷活动”不仅是与地雷相关——它还开启了以个人微薄之力与政府合作的新方式。

我坚信自己的权利和职责可以开创一个新的世界，在那个世界里，不会美化暴力和战争，可以寻求不同的方法去解决一些常见的问题。我坚信，到那时候，你将敢于发表你的看法，敢于从不同的资源找到想要的信息，敢于将一切付诸实践。

我深知，有如此信念并敢于在公众面前表达出来，不是一件令人好过的容易事，也不总是受欢迎的——尤其是在“9.11”之后的世界。但我相信，生活不是一场声誉竞赛。我真的不在乎那些对我如潮的评价。对于我来说，只是在朝着正确的方向前进——即使无人旁观。

我相信，只是担心世界末日、星球毁灭而不采取行动是毫无用处的。改变世界的唯一途径就是：行动。

大部分人往往会陷入“一定要上大学”的怪圈，然后找到工作，贷款买房。不知怎么，我就是鬼使神差般地想做一些不寻常的事情。

the drive—to do things a bit differently.

I believe that words are easy—the truth is told in the actions we take. If enough ordinary people back up our desire for a better world with action, I believe we can, in fact, accomplish extraordinary things.

我也相信“说到容易做到难”的道理。如果有足够的普通人愿意为创造一个更好的世界而行动起来，我相信我们能够做到，并且是用平凡人的身份去完成非凡的梦想！

活出最真的自我

Birds sing after a storm. Why shouldn't people feel as free to delight in whatever sunlight remains to them?

—— Rose KennedyI

鸟儿在暴风雨后歌唱，人们为什么在仍是阳光普照的时候还不尽情感受快乐呢?

——罗丝・肯尼迪

Putting in a Good Word for Guilt

为内疚正名

◎ Ellen Goodman

Feeling guilty is nothing to feel guilty about. Yes, guilt can be the excess baggage that keeps us paralyzed unless we dump it. But it can also be the engine that fuels us. Yes, it can be a self-punishing activity, but it can also be the conscience that keeps us civilized.

Not too long ago I wrote a story about that amusing couple Guilt and the Working Mother. I'll tell you more about that later. Through the mail someone sent me a gift coffee mug carrying the message "I gave up guilt for Lent."

My first reaction was to giggle. But then it occurred to me that this particular Lent has been too lengthy. For the past decade or more, the pop psychologists who use book jackets rather than couches all were busy telling us that I am okay, you are okay and whatever we do is okay.

In most of their books, guilt was given a bad name—or rather, an assortment of bad names. It was a (1) Puritan (2) Jewish (3) Catholic hangover from our (1) parents (2) culture (3) religion. To be truly liberated was to be

作者简介

埃伦·古德曼（Ellen Goodman，1941—），美国记者，曾获普利策奖的知名专栏作家。曾在《新闻周刊》《底特律自由报》《波士顿全球报》担任记者，已出版多部作品。

内疚感与感觉内疚并不能相提并论。是的，内疚会成为超负荷的包袱，除非我们卸下这种包袱，否则我们终会筋疲力竭。但是，内疚也可以成为我们前进的动力。是的，内疚可以是一种自我惩罚的行为，但它也可以是一种道德心，以保持我们的文明开化。

不久前，我写过一个故事，讲的是内疚和职业母亲这对有趣的搭档。我会在下文中告知你们她们的后续故事。有人给我邮寄了一个礼物，是一个写有“我为大斋节放弃内疚感”字样的咖啡杯。

我的第一反应便是觉得好笑。但随后我便想起，这个特殊的大斋节时间太长。在过去的十年或者更长时间里，通俗心理学工作者都在忙着使用书籍封套而非心理诊室来告诉我们，你好，我好，做什么都好。

在他们所出的大部分书籍中，内疚都背负着恶名——或者近似恶名的名称。它是（1）清教（2）犹太教（3）天主教的遗留观念，源自我们的（1）父母（2）文化和（3）宗教。真正的无拘无束是要摆脱内疚感，无论这种内疚感是来自富有、权势、名望、不孝、轻率，还是迟到、吸烟

free of guilt about being rich, powerful, number one, bad to your mother, thoughtless, late, a smoker or about cheating on your spouse.

There was a popular notion, in fact, that self-love began by slaying one's guilt. People all around us spent a great portion of the last decade trying to tune out guilt instead of decoding its message and learning what it was trying to tell us.

With that sort of success, guilt was ripe for revival. Somewhere along the I'm-okay-you're-okay way, many of us realized that, in fact, I am not always okay and neither are you. Furthermore, we did not want to join the legions who conquered their guilt en route to new depths of narcissistic rottenness.

At the deepest, most devastating level, guilt is the criminal in us that longs to be caught. It is the horrible, pit-of-the-stomach sense of having done wrong. It is, as Lady Macbeth obsessively knew, the spot that no one else may see…and we can't see around.

To be without guilt is to be without a conscience. Guilt-free people don't feel bad when they cause pain to others, and so they go on guilt-freely causing more pain. The last thing we need more of is less conscience.

Freud once said, "As regards conscience, God has done an uneven and careless piece of work, for a large majority of men have brought along with them only a modest amount of it, or scarcely enough to be worth mentioning."

Now, I am not suggesting that we all sign up for a new guilt trip. But there has to be some line between the accusation that we all should feel guilty for, say, poverty or racism and the assertion that the oppressed have "chosen"

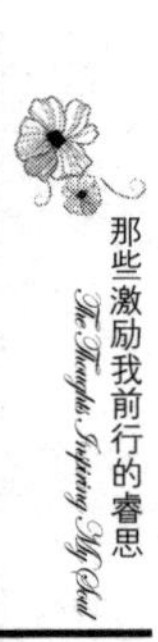

或者出轨。

实际上，之前有个很流行的观点说，自爱始于消除自己的内疚感。我们周围的所有人将以往十年的大部分时间都用于逃避内疚感，而不是破解其含义，去探究内疚一直想要告诉我们的信息。

逃避成功之后，内疚便获得了成熟的复活时机。沿着你好我好的大道一直往前走，我们之中有很多人都意识到，其实我并非一直都很好，你也不是。此外，我们并不想加入这样的军团，用一种深层次的自我陶醉式的堕落，去克服自己的内疚感。

在那最深层、最具毁灭性的层面上，内疚感成为了我们内心一个渴望被捕获的罪犯。它是那种堵在胸口的极其讨厌的犯错感。这就像是困扰着麦克白夫人的那种感受，一个其他人看不到的污点……而我们自己还不能侧头四顾。

没有内疚感就没有道德心。没有内疚感的人在伤害他人之后不会觉得难受，因此他们就会毫不内疚地造成更多的伤害。我们最不需要的便是丧失道德心。

弗洛伊德曾说："说到道德心，上帝在这件事上既不公平也不仔细，因为，有很大一部分人生来就未带有足量的道德心，甚至少到不值一提。"

说到这里，我并不是建议大家都报名参加一次新的内疚之旅。但是，以下两种论断之间是有分别的：一者认为我们应该为贫穷或种族主义感到内疚，一者断言这些受压迫者都是"命中注定"。

清教主义和享乐主义之间肯定存在着某种更为中立的主义。有些父

their lot in life.

There has to be something between puritanism and hedonism. There has to be something between the parents who guilt-trip their children across every stage of life and those who offer no guidance, no—gulp—moral or ethical point of view.

At quite regular intervals, for example, my daughter looks up at me in the midst of a discussion (she would call it a lecture) and says: "You're making me feel guilty." For a long time this made me, in turn, feel guilty. But now I realize that I am doing precisely what I am supposed to be doing: instilling in her a sense of right and wrong so that she will feel uncomfortable if she behaves in hurtful ways.

This is, of course, a very tricky business. Guilt is ultimately the way we judge ourselves. It is the part of us that says, "I deserve to be punished." But we all know people who feel guilty just for being alive. We know people who are paralyzed by irrational guilt. And we certainly don't want to be among them, or to shepherd our children into their flock.

But it seems to me that the trick isn't to become flaccidly nonjudgemental, but to figure out whether we are being fair judges of ourselves. Karl Menninger once wrote that one aim of psychiatric treatment isn't to get rid of guilt but "to get people's guilt feelings attached to the 'right' things."

In his book Feelings, Willard Gaylin quotes a Reverend Tillotson's definition of guilt as "nothing else but trouble arising in our mind from our

母在其孩子生命的每个阶段都教导他们要有内疚感，而有的父母却没有任何的指导，也从不教给孩子一丁点道德伦理方面的观念，这两个极端之间肯定存在着更加恰当的教育方法。

按照常规，在此举个例子，我的女儿在一次讨论（她也许会将其称为教训）时抬头望着我说："你让我觉得很内疚。"但是反过来，这句话在很长一段时间里都让我觉得很内疚。但是现在我意识到，这就是我所应该做的事情：给她输入一种是非观，这样，当她在伤害他人之后才会觉得心里不安。

当然，这是一件很讲究技巧的事情。从根本上说，内疚是我们进行自我评价的一种方式。它是我们内心的一部分在说："我理应受到惩罚。"但是，我们都知道，有些人单纯因为活着都感觉内疚。我们还知道，有些人被一些荒谬的内疚感折腾得筋疲力尽。而我们自然不会想要成为他们中的一员，也不想自己的孩子加入他们的行列。

但对我来说，技巧并不在于软弱得没有个人的道德标准，而是要搞清楚我们在进行自我评价时是否公正。卡尔·门宁格尔曾写道，精神病治疗的目的并不是摆脱内疚，而是"让人们的内疚感依附于'正确'的事情"。

维勒德·盖林在他的书《情感》中，引用了牧师蒂洛森对于内疚的定义："内疚不是别物，而是当我们意识到自己的所作所为违背了自身职责时，在我们心中所产生的苦恼。"

但是，我们对于职责却有着各种各样的认知。一个月前，我与两位

consciousness of having done contrary to what we are verily persuaded was our Duty."

We may, however, have wildly different senses of duty. I had lunch with two friends a month ago when they both started talking about feeling guilty for neglecting their mothers. One, it turned out, worried that she didn't call "home" every day; the other hadn't even chatted with her mother since Christmas.

We are also particularly vulnerable to feelings of duty in a time of change. Today an older and ingrained sense of what we should do may conflict with a new one. In the gaps that open between what we once were taught and what we now believe grows a rich crop of guilt.

Mothers now often tell me that they feel guilty if they are working and guilty if they aren't. One set of older expectations, to be a perfect milk-and-cookies supermom, conflicts with another, to be an independent woman or an economic helpmate.

But duty has its uses. It sets us down at the typewriter, hustles us to the job on a morning when everything has gone wrong, pushes us toward the crying baby at 3 A.M.

If guilt is a struggle between our acceptance of shoulds and should nots, it is a powerful and intensely human one. Gaylin writes, "Guilt represents the noblest and most painful of struggles. It is between us and ourselves." It is better to struggle with ourselves than give up on ourselves.

This worst emotion, in a sense, helps bring out the best in us. The desire to avoid feeling guilty makes us avoid the worst sort of behavior. The early

朋友共进午餐，当时她们都提到自己忽视了自己的母亲，因而觉得心里不安。结果，她们其中一个担心的是自己没有每天打电话“回家”，另一个是因为从圣诞节过后就没和母亲聊过天。

在这个充满了变化的时代，我们特别容易感觉到身上的责任。今天，对于我们该做什么、不该做什么，一个根深蒂固的旧观念也许会与新观念产生冲突。在我们过去所受的教育和现在的认知之间，存在着一条洞开的鸿沟，里面衍生出了各种各样的内疚感。

现在常有母亲告诉我说，如果工作的话会觉得过意不去，不工作还是过意不去。老一套的观念告诉我们，要做一个会烘焙完美奶油饼干的超级妈妈，另一个与之相左的观念认为，要做一个独立的女人，一个有经济能力的配偶。

但是，职责有其自身的用途。它让我们安坐于打字机前，催促我们在一个万事不顺的早晨去上班，说服我们在凌晨 3 点起床安抚哭泣的婴孩。

如果内疚感是我们接受该做什么与不该做什么之间的一种挣扎，那它就是一种强大而且极富人性的情感。盖林写道：“内疚感代表了最为崇高且最为痛苦的挣扎。这是我们与自己的斗争。”与自己斗争总比对自己绝望好。

在某种程度上，这种最糟糕的情感有助于激发我们内心最美好的一面。避免感到内疚的渴望会让我们避开那些最糟糕的言行。一个孩子伤害了弟弟或妹妹，即便无人知晓也觉得内疚，这就是一个很好的开端。

guilt of a child who has hurt a younger sister or brother, even when no one else knows, is a message. The adult who has inflicted pain on an innocent, who has cheated, lied, stolen, to get ahead of another—each of us has a list—wakes up in the middle of the night and remembers it.

In that sense guilt is the great civilizer, the internal commandment that helps us choose to be kind to each other rather than to join in a stampede of me-firsts. "If guilt is coming back," said Harvard Professor David Riesman, who wrote The Lonely Crowd, "one reason is that a tremendous surge of young people overpowered the adults in the sixties. You might say the barbarians took Rome. Now there are more adults around who are trying to restore some stability."

Guilt is the adult in each of us, the parent, the one who upholds the standards. It is the internal guide against which we argue in vain that "everybody else is doing it."

We even wrestle with ethical dilemmas and conflicts of conscience so that we can live with ourselves more comfortably. I know two people who were faced with a crisis about their infidelities. One woman resolved the triangle she was in by ending her marriage. The other ended her affair. In both cases, it was the pain that had motivated them to change.

It is not easy to attach our guilt to the right things. It is never easy to separate right from wrong, rational guilt from neurotic guilt. We may resolve one by changing our view of it and another by changing our behavior.

In my own life as a working mother, I have done both half a dozen times.

成年人如果让一个无辜的人承受了痛苦，为了超越他人而欺骗、撒谎、偷窃——我们每个人心里都有一张清单——那他总会在半夜醒来，一切都记忆犹新。

这样看来，内疚感是伟大的文明助推器，是我们内心的戒条，帮助我们选择与人为善，而不是与那些“利己主义”拥作一团。“如果内疚感复苏，”《孤独的人群》作者、哈佛大学的大卫·里斯曼教授说，“原因之一便是在 60 年代，年轻人的巨大浪潮压过了成年人。你也可以说是野蛮人占领了罗马。但是现在周围的成年人越来越多，他们都在试着恢复稳定的局面。”

内疚感是我们每个人心中的成年人，是父母，是那些维持标准的人。它是我们内心的指导者，反对我们一直以来徒劳争辩的“其他人都这么做的”。

我们甚至试图解决伦理困境和道德冲突，这样我们就能过得更舒服一些。我认识两个人，她们因为自己的出轨而面临着婚姻危机。其中一个通过离婚结束了三角关系，另一个结束了自己的婚外情。在这两个案例中，都是痛苦在驱使她们进行改变。

想要将内疚感依附在正确的事情上并不容易。从来就很难区分正确与错误，也很难分清理性的内疚和神经质的内疚。我可以通过改变自己的观念解决其中一个，再通过改变自己的行为解决另一个。

在我作为一个上班母亲的那段时间，这两种方法我都试过好多次。那时我的女儿还小，而我在上班，我担心我不能像我自己的妈妈一样做

When my daughter was small and I was working, I worried that I was not following the pattern of the good mother, my mother. Only through time and perspective and reality did I change that view; I realized that my daughter clearly did not feel neglected and I clearly was not uncaring. Good child care, love, luck and support helped me to resolve my early guilt feelings.

Then again, last winter I found myself out of town more than I was comfortable with. This time I changed my schedule instead of my mind.

For all of us, in the dozens of daily decisions we make, guilt is one of the many proper motivations. I am not saying our lives are ruled by guilt. Hardly. But guilt is inherent in the underlying question: “If I do that, can I live with myself?”

People who don’t ask themselves that question, people who never get no for an answer, may seem lucky. They can, we think, be self-centered without self-punishment, hedonistic without qualms. They can worry about me-first and forget about the others.

It is easy to be jealous of those who go through life without a moment of wrenching guilt. But envying the guiltless is like envying a house pet. Striving to follow their lead is like accepting a catatonic as your role model. They are not the free but the antisocial. In a world in which guilt is one of the few emotions experienced only by human beings, they are, even, unhuman.

Guilt is one of the most human of dilemmas. It is the claim of others on the self, the recognition both of our flaws and of our desire to be the people we want to be.

个好妈妈。直到后来，随着时间、思考问题的角度和现实的变化，我才改变了这个观念。我知道我的女儿完全没有觉得自己被忽视了，而我也完全不是不予关怀的妈妈。给予孩子关心、爱护、机会和支持，这些都帮助我解决了早期的内疚感。

去年冬天，我发现自己外出的时候越来越多，心中再次觉得有些不安。这次，我改变了自己的行程，而不是观念。

我们所有人每天都会做很多决定，而大多数情况下，都是内疚感在驱使我们做这样的决定。我并不是说我们的生活受到内疚感的控制。完全不是这样。但是，内疚感一直都位于这样一个潜在问题之中："如果我那么做了，我能安心吗？"

那些不会问自己这个问题的人，那些答案永远是"能安心"的人，似乎非常幸运。在我们看来，他们能够摆脱自我惩罚做到以自我为中心，不用忍受良心的谴责而享受快乐。他们挂虑的是首先利己，而将他人抛诸脑后。

有些人一生都不曾有一刻钟受到内疚的折磨，这很容易让我们嫉妒。但是，嫉妒这些不内疚的人就像嫉妒一只家养宠物。努力追随他们的脚步，就像是把一名精神病患者作为你的榜样。他们并非无拘无束，而是危害社会安宁之人。在这样一个世界里，内疚感是只有人类才能体验到几种情感之一，而他们根本就不是人。

内疚感是最具人性的窘境之一。它是时刻为他人考虑，认识到自己的缺点和渴求，成为我们想要成为的人。

Of Envy
论嫉妒

◎ Francis Bacon

There be none of the affections, which have been noted to fascinate or bewitch, but love and envy. They both have vehement wishes; they frame themselves readily into imaginations and suggestions; and they come easily into the eye, especially upon the present of the objects; which are the points that conduce to fascination, if any such thing there be. We see likewise, the Scripture calleth envy an evil eye; and the astrologers, call the evil influences of the stars, evil aspects; so that still there seemeth to be acknowledged, in the act of envy, an ejaculation or irradiation of the eye.

Nay, some have been so curious, as to note, that the times when the stroke or percussion of an envi-ous eye doth most hurt, are when the party envied is beheld in glory or triumph; for that sets an edge upon envy: and besides, at such times the spirits of the person envied, do come forth most into the outward parts, and so meet the blow.

But leaving these curiosities (though not un-worthy to be thought on, in fit place), we will handle, what persons are apt to envy others; what persons are most subject to be envied themselves; and what is the difference between

除了爱与嫉妒，世上再无什么情感能让人迷醉或神魂颠倒。这两者都包含有热烈的渴望，它们乐意自己被束缚在想象力和细微迹象的条框之中。它们很容易落入世人眼中，尤其是那些被爱和被嫉妒的人眼中。如果这世上真有迷恋存在的话，这些都是导致迷恋的要点。我们同样可以看到，经文圣典中常把嫉妒称为邪眼，而占星家常把星星邪恶的影响力称为凶兆，以致世人现在还承认，嫉妒发生之时，嫉妒者会目露寒光。

有些人非常喜欢追根刨底，竟然注意到，嫉妒之眼在被嫉妒者正志得意满时最为伤人，因为这种情绪会让嫉妒火焰烧至极致：而且，此时被嫉妒者的得意情绪会不禁喜形于色，正好与嫉妒之火发生碰撞。

但是，先撇开这些好奇心（并不是说这些好奇心不值得在适当的场合考虑一下），我们一起来探讨一下什么样的人易于嫉妒他人，什么样的人最容易招来嫉妒，以及公众嫉妒和私人嫉妒之间的区别。

一个自身没有德行之人，易于嫉妒他人之德行。因为滋养人心要么有赖于自身行善，要么有赖于他人行恶。缺乏并且想要自身德行的人会

public and private envy.

A man that hath no virtue in himself, ever en-vieth virtue in others. For men's minds, will either feed upon their own good, or upon others' evil; and who wanteth the one, will prey upon the other; and whoso is out of hope, to attain to another's virtue, will seek to come at even hand, by depress-ing another's fortune.

A man that is busy, and inquisitive, is com-monly envious. For to know much of other men's matters, cannot be because all that ado may con-cern his own estate; therefore it must needs be, that he taketh a kind of play-pleasure, in looking upon the fortunes of others. Neither can he, that mindeth but his own business, find much matter for envy. For envy is a gadding passion, and walk-eth the streets, and doth not keep home: Non est curiosus, quin idem sit malevolus.

Men of noble birth, are noted to be envious towards new men, when they rise. For the distance is altered, and it is like a deceit of the eye, that when others come on, they think themselves, go back.

Deformed persons, and eunuchs, and old men, and bastards, are envious. For he that cannot pos-sibly mend his own case, will do what he can, to impair another's; except these defects light upon a very brave, and heroical nature, which thinketh to make his natural wants part of his honor; in that it should be said, that an eunuch, or a lame man, did such great matters; affecting the honor of a miracle; as it was in Narses the eunuch, and Agesi-laus and Tamberlanes, that were lame men.

掠食他人之德行。而那些无望获得他人德行之人，便会通过贬低他人的善行来寻求平衡。

那种好管闲事且好打听的人，常常是好嫉妒之人。因为打探他人大量的信息不可能都是因为这些事与自身有利害关系，因此，这定是因为他能在旁观他人运势之时享有一种戏剧般的乐趣。如果他一心只管自家的琐事，便不能找到这么多可嫉妒的事情。因为嫉妒是一种闲荡的热情，而且总爱在街上游荡，不喜呆在家里：好事者必定居心不良。

生就贵族的人在新人晋升封爵时常生嫉妒。因为俩人之间差距的缩短，而这就像是视觉发生了错觉，会把他人获得的提升看成自己爵位的降低。

残疾人、宦官、老人、私生子都易于嫉妒。因为他们无法弥补自身的缺陷，所以就会想方设法地损害他人。除非这些有缺陷的人拥有非常勇敢无畏的英雄本性，能够将其固有的缺陷转变成其荣誉的一部分。这样一来，人们就会说：某个宦官或某个瘸子创下了丰功伟业，赢得了奇迹般的荣誉。就像人们谈论宦官纳西斯、瘸子阿杰西雷斯和帖木儿那样。

Silence Is Golden

静谧之夜，沉默是金

◎ Fred Burks

About five years ago, I started making it a top priority to set aside one evening a week as time to myself. Not long afterwards, I found myself using these evenings as a time of silence, reflection, and **meditation**[①]—a time to open to my own inner wisdom. My spiritual nature began pulling me deep into myself, so that before long, I called these times my evenings of silence.

I soon developed guidelines for my weekly evenings of silence, which I continue to use to this day. I do not use this time to read, work on the computer, or do anything that might distract me from moving within. I only write if it is to record an **inspiration**[②] I receive during these times. I often play soft, recorded music which supports me on my inward journey. I do my best to pay attention to my breath, as I've found slow, deep breaths greatly assist me in calming my thoughts and feeling my connection with my deeper self and

① meditation [.medi'teiʃən] n. 沉思；冥想

② inspiration [.inspə'reiʃən] n. 灵感，鼓舞人心（的东西）；吸气

大约 5 年前，我开始每周留出一晚上作为我自己的时间，并把它看做是最重要的事。不久以后，我发现自己开始把这些静谧的夜晚用来思考、冥想，开启内心的智慧。我的精神力量开始把自己拉向内心深处，因此，没过多久，我就把这些夜晚称为“静谧之夜”。

我很快就为每周的“静谧之夜”制定出一套准则，并且直到今天仍在沿用。在这段时间里，我不能看书、用电脑或者做其他一些干扰思绪向内探索的事情。如果要记录此时突然闪过的灵感，我只能写下来。我常会播放事先录好的轻柔的音乐，来帮助我踏上向内心探寻的旅程。我努力注意我的呼吸，因为我发现，缓慢而深长的呼吸能极大地帮助我平静心绪，感受与内心深处的自我和精神之间的联结。

每当我开始“静谧之夜”时，我会拿出 10 到 15 分钟，让我的思绪随意游走。我的思绪通常需要漫无目的地游荡，也需要思考当天发生的

with Spirit.

When I start an evening of silence, I usually set aside 10 to 15 minutes to allow my mind to go wherever it wants to go. My mind usually needs to wander and to process what's been going on during the day, so I give it full permission to do so during this time. Yet even while doing this, I continue to focus on slow, deep breaths, reminding me of my intention to go deeper.

Either at the beginning of the evening, or after this time of allowing my mind to run freely, I move into silent prayer asking for help and guidance in bringing me to a place of deep connection and inspiration. I also choose a topic from my life for **contemplation**[①] this evening as I send up these prayers. I end this prayer by reaffirming my commitment to what's best for all, to divine guidance, and to love, support, and empower all to be the best that we can be.

How I use the remainder of my time in silence has shifted over the years. When I first started, I did a number of exercises which helped me to move deeper. I would spend some time doing deep, rapid breaths while asking for guidance before moving back into slow, deep breaths. I would sit in front of a mirror looking deep into my own eyes while inviting myself to open to loving myself deeply. I would **hum**[②] a single note (toning) with the intention of moving more deeply into connection with myself and with the Divine.

More recently, however, I only occasionally use these practices. I have become much better at surrendering to guidance from my inner self and from

① contemplation [.kɔntem'peiʃən] n. 注视；沉思；打算
② hum [hʌm] v. 发低哼声；哼（曲子）；活跃

事情，因此我完全允许它在这段时间里任意遐想。但是，即使在这段时间，我也会继续关注自己缓慢而深长的呼吸，提醒自己向内心深处投射注意力。

无论是每个“静谧之夜”开始时，还是在思绪任意游走之后，我都会静静地祈祷，希望获得帮助和指导，能让自己进入深层联结和灵感所在之处。在祈祷时，我也会从生活中选择一个当晚冥想的主题。我一再重申我的义务，以此来结束我的祈祷，这些义务是致力于最美好的事物、忠于神的指引、忠于爱和支持，以及为我们每个人能达到最好状态而贡献力量。

至于如何使用“静谧之夜”剩下来的时间，在这些年里，我总是在不断变化着。最开始的时候，我会做些运动来让自己进入状态。在寻求指引时，我会花时间做些深长但又快速的呼吸，而后又回到深长且缓慢的呼吸。我会坐在镜子前面，深深地凝望着自己的眼睛，引导自己打开心扉，去更深地爱自己。我也会低声哼个小曲，让自己进入内心更深处，体会与自我的联结，以及与神的联结。

然而，最近我只是偶尔会使用这些方法。我能更好地听从来自内在自我和精神的指引，因此，我可以不使用以上方法就自然地进入内心深处。但是我依然认为，缓慢而深长的呼吸非常重要，为这些特别时段设

Spirit, so that I naturally go deep without the aid of the above practices. I do, however, continue to place great importance in slow, deep breaths, and in setting an intention for what I want to explore in these special times.

I find these evenings of silence incredibly refreshing and rejuvenating! It is so wonderful and **empowering**[①] to have this time to remind myself of the deeper reasons for why I am here and what I am doing with my life. It's like getting recharged and refocused every week so that I can move more clearly and powerfully through the rest of the week. I have so enjoyed it, in fact, that I started doing occasional full days of silence. Two years ago, I even decided to set aside five consecutive days once a year for deep silence and contemplation. Though these times certainly can bring up challenges, in the end they are almost always incredibly inspiring and empowering.

For anyone interested in getting to know your inner world better and in developing a stronger, deeper connection with the Divine, I highly recommend exploring time in silence on a regular basis. You will be amazed at the amount of wisdom you hold within yourself if only you are willing to be patient and to open fully to your own deeper self. It has clearly been one of the most powerful ways I've found to continue to grow, learn, and find ever more love, joy, and empowerment in my life.

① empower [im'pauə] v. 授权；使能够

定我想要探索的目标也至关重要。

我发现这些“静谧之夜”给我带来了难以置信的清新感受和充沛活力。拥有这段时间来提醒我自己为什么会在这里、我在做什么，这是多么美妙而鼓舞人心！这就像每周充电一次，并重新聚焦生活的核心一样，这样，我就可以目标更清晰、更有力量地度过那周剩下的日子。我是如此享受，事实上，我后来开始偶尔尝试整天沉默冥想。两年前，我甚至决定拿出一年中连续五天时间来进行深度沉默和冥想。尽管这些时间会有一些挑战，但最终它们几乎总是难以置信地给我带来灵感和力量。

对于任何想要更好地了解自己的内心世界，与神建立更坚固、深刻的联结的人，我极力推荐定期的冥想方法——在静谧时刻向内心探索。只要你足够有耐心，并愿意向内心的自我完全开放，你将会为自己内心保有的智慧而惊叹不已。我发现，这显然是在生命中继续成长、学习，并找到更多爱、喜悦和力量的最有效的方式之一。

The Lost Art of Giving
遗失的艺术——奉献

◎ Mary Jaksch

The season of giving is upon us. We know about the benefits of giving to the one who receives. They feel appreciated, loved, understood and so on.

But what about the benefits of giving to the one who gives?

The other day, I had an interesting experience at the supermarket. An elderly man stepped towards me, offered me a twenty cent piece and said, "I'm Greg. Would you like twenty cents towards buying food for the local Foodbank?" It turned out that he's a Rotary member and was trying to encourage people to buy food for those who live in poverty.

I immediately dropped my own grocery plans and decided to shop for the Foodbank instead. I bought pasta, tomato sauce, cans of beans, a couple of packs of cereal, a Christmas pudding and some other bits and pieces. I imagined how a family in need would feel when they enjoyed my Christmas pudding, or how a mother would be happy to put breakfast in front of hungry kids. When I handed over my shopping bags to Greg, his face split in a big

作者简介

玛丽·杰克斯（Mary Jaksch），著名心理治疗师，冥想导师，作家，现居住于新西兰。代表作《关于爱的一切》（*All About Love*）已被译为 7 种语言发行。

奉献的节日快到了。我们都知道给予为获赠人带来很多益处，他们会感受到欣赏、关爱和理解等等。

但是，奉献对于给予者来说有什么益处呢？

几天前，我在一家超市经历了一件耐人寻味的事情。在我挑选商品的时候，一位老人朝我走来，递给我一枚 20 美分的硬币，对我说道："我叫格雷格，你愿意用这 20 美分在这里的一家食物银行里购物么？"他自称他是一名扶轮社（译者注：一个国际性的慈善组织）的成员，正在鼓励人们为一些穷人奉献食物。

我立马就改变了在那家超市的购物计划，转而去了食物银行。我在那里买了意粉、蕃茄酱、豆类罐头、几袋麦片、一个圣诞布丁和其他一些零零碎碎的东西。我想象着，一户忍饥挨饿的家庭在吃我的圣诞布丁时会感到什么样的滋味，还有，一位母亲把早饭端给她那饥肠辘辘的孩子时会多么幸福。我把购物袋交给格雷格时，他咧嘴笑了，而我的眼珠却湿润了。从那以后，我开始思考，为什么奉献能触动心灵中最柔软的

grin. Tears gathered in my eyes. Afterward I wondered why giving touches the heart.

Giving moves us because it frees us.

For a moment we are released from thoughts about how we are, how we were, how we will be, how people see us, how we could be, how we should be, and so on. It's what my teacher Robert Aitken calls the "Me-tape", the tape that keeps on playing in our mind.

When we give with an open heart, we remember that we are not alone.

You may want to say to me, "What? Of course I know I'm not alone!"

True. But let's try an experiment. In order for this experiment to work, you need to be stressed. You're not? Congratulations, you're obviously a saint and can stop reading now. The experiment is for the rest of us who hurtle towards Christmas. We try to complete work, buy Christmas presents, attend work functions, organise the holidays, plan celebrations, contact family and friends, clean the home, and do many other things—even though time seems to accelerate.

Ok, so you and I are stressed, right? My question to you is: When stressed, what percentage of waking time do you spend thinking about your own life?

Include thoughts about your work, planning thoughts, thoughts about the past, thoughts about pressing tasks, and thoughts about your relationship with others.

Well, what's the percentage? It's high, isn't it?

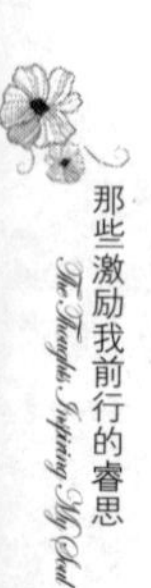

部分。

奉献感动我们，因为它使我们自由。

在奉献的时候，我们会从我们现在如何、我们过去如何、我们将会如何、别人如何看我们、我们能改变什么、我们应该怎么样等等诸如此类的思虑烦扰中脱离出来。我的老师罗伯特·艾特肯把这些思想称为“自我磁带”，它一直在我们的脑海里循环播放。

当我们敞开心门去奉献时，我们会发觉自己并不是单独一人。

你也许会反驳我：“什么？我自然不是一个人！”

确实如此。但让我们先来做个试验。为了使试验有效，你需要感到压力。你没有？那么恭喜你，很显然，你是一个十足的圣人，可以不用读下去了。这个试验是为我们当中的凡夫俗子所准备的。尽管时间好像在加速溜走，我们还是要努力完成工作，购买圣诞节礼物，参加工作会议，设计出游和庆祝方案，接触家人和朋友，打扫房间，林林总总，诸如此类。

有这么多的事情要做，你和我是否倍感压力呢？那么，我给你的问题是：

当你感到压力重重时，你会在走路的时候花多少时间思考你的人生？

你会思考你的工作，你的计划，你的过去，你就要做的任务，你与他人的关系等等。

你看，思考这些问题是不是占用了你很大一部分的时间？

The higher the stress, the more we become **wrapped up in**[1] our own life.

And when we're wrapped up in our own life, we become oblivious to the fact that there are others "out there", and that they have problems and needs too. That's where the miracle of giving comes in. When we give with an open heart, we suddenly wake up from the "Me-tape" and feel connected to others.

When we give with a pure heart, we feel joyful.

What is a pure heart? It's giving with no thought of return. In reality, our motives for giving are often tinged with "impure" motives: maybe we are shamed or intimidated into giving; or we give to receive a favour; or we give in order to feel good about ourselves. Is "impure" giving worthless? I don't think so. Every action is in some way "impure" because we are human beings, and not saints.

At the core of each one of us, there is a goodness yearning to find expression.

Each act of giving emerges from that core of goodness, even though layers of mixed motivation may cloud our natural **aspiration**[2] of generosity. Whenever we touch that core of goodness, we feel moved. This is natural giving.

---

① wrap up in 醉心于……，沉浸于……

② aspiration [æspə'reɪʃ(ə)n] n. 渴望；抱负

我们受到的压力越大，我们就越容易沉浸在自己的世界之中。

当我们沉醉于自己的生活之中时，我们就会无视他人的存在，然而，这些人也有自己的难处和需要。奉献会在此显现出它的奇妙来。我们敞开心门奉献时，就会瞬间从“自我磁带”中回过神来，发觉其实有很多人围绕在自己的身边。

当我们用真心奉献时，我们便喜乐满溢。

什么是真心奉献？当我们在奉献时不曾想有任何回报，这就是真心的奉献。现实中，我们的奉献总是蒙上了一层不洁的动机：也许我们羞于或被迫去奉献；或是我们想要得到帮助；或是我们想提升自己的好感。那么，这些奉献都是无价值的吗？我不这么认为。不可否认的是，我们的一举一动，在某种意义上来说都带着不洁的动机。这很正常，因为我们只是普通人，不是圣人。

在我们的最深处，我们的善心正在有力地跳动。

虽然形形色色的动机掩盖了我们最自然地表现慷慨的渴望，但每一次的奉献都是从善心而起的。无论什么时候，当我们触摸自己的善心时，我们就会感动。这就是最纯真的奉献。

The Kindness of Strangers

陌生人的善行

◎ Robert Levine

Two images: First, as a 6-year-old boy growing up in New York City, I am walking with my father on a crowded midtown street. The rush of pedestrians suddenly **backs up**[①] before me as people narrow into a single lane to avoid a large object on the sidewalk. To my astonishment, the object turns out to be a human being lying unconscious against a building. My father quickly points to a bottle in a paper bag next to him. Not one of the passing herd seems to actually notice the man—certainly, none make eye contact—as they robotically follow the makeshift **detour**[②]. My father, who I look up to as a model loving, caring man, explains that the poor soul on the sidewalk "just needs to sleep it off." When the prone man suddenly begins to ramble senselessly, my father stops me. "You never know how he'll react." I later came to see these two teachings—"there's nothing you can do" and "try not to

① back up 支持，援助；（资料）备份；倒退

② detour ['diːtʊə] n. 绕道

作者简介

罗伯特·莱文（Robert Levine），美国加州大学弗雷斯诺分校心理学教授。他的教学及研究已获诸多奖项，其作品在《今日心理学》《发现》等众多媒体杂志发表。现担任西方心理学协会主席。

我先讲讲我的两次记忆：第一次发生在我6岁时。那时我在纽约，有一天，我和父亲走在市中心一条拥挤的街道上。突然，我前面的人群纷纷往后退，挤到了一条小道上，来躲避人行道上一个庞大的物体。我惊讶地发现，这个物体原来是一个人，他正迷迷糊糊地躺在一栋房子旁边。我父亲马上指了一下他旁边纸袋里的一个瓶子。在他身边路过的人好像没有一个人注意到他，他们瞅都没瞅他一眼，就这样机械地跟着前面的人，将就着从他旁边绕了过去。我的父亲一直被我视作善良友善之人，他告诉我说，这个可怜的人也许只是想找个地方睡一觉。突然，这个趴着的人无意识地摆动了下手脚，我正想过去帮忙，父亲阻止了我：“你不知道他要做什么的。”稍后，我从这件事上学到了两句话——“你什么也做不了”和“不要自找麻烦”，这两句话从此变成了我在城市里

get involved"—as my anthems of urban survival.

Next, fast forward several years to a market in Rangoon, Burma (now Myanmar). I had spent the previous 12 months travelling in poor Asian cities, but even by those standards this was a scene of misery. Besides the **inconceivable**[①] poverty, it is sweltering hot, ridiculously crowded and the wind is blowing dust everywhere. Suddenly, a man carrying a huge bag of peanuts calls out in pain and falls to the ground. I then witness an astonishing piece of choreography. Appearing to have rehearsed the scene many times, a half dozen sellers run from their stalls to help, leaving unattended what may be the totality of their possessions. One puts a blanket under the man's head, another opens his shirt, a third questions him carefully about the pain, a fourth gets water, a fifth keeps onlookers from crowding too close, a sixth runs for a doctor. Within minutes, the doctor arrives, and two other locals join in to assist. The performance could have passed for a final exam at paramedic school.

Rousseau once wrote that "cities are the sink of the human race." But as my experiences in New York and Rangoon made clear, no two cities are the same. Places, like individuals, have their own personalities.

In what cities is a needy stranger more likely to receive help? What sort of community teaches a citizen to withhold **compassion**[②] toward strangers? As a grown-up social psychologist, I have spent much of the past two decades

① inconceivable [ɪnkən'si:vəb(ə)l] adj. 不可思议的；难以置信的

② compassion [kəm'pæʃ(ə)n] n. 同情；怜悯

生存的金玉良言。

还有一次，是几年后发生在缅甸首都仰光的一个市场里的一件事。在此之前，我已经在这些亚洲的贫穷城市里旅行了 12 个月，但这座城市的光景更为凄凉，到处都弥漫着悲哀困苦。除了极端的贫穷外，仰光还特别闷热，街道上挤满了人，风带着沙子呼啸在这座城市的每一个角落。忽然之间，一个背着一大袋花生的男人痛苦地大叫一声，随即就倒在了地上。随后，我目睹了一个不可思议的场景。好像是彩排了无数次一样，六个小贩从他们的摊位上跑出来帮忙，也不理会那些可能是他们所有身家的货物。一个小贩把一块毯子枕在那个男人下面，还有一个解开他的衣襟，第三个人详细地询问他的病情，第四个人端来了一杯水，第五个阻止那些围观者靠得太近，第六个跑去叫医生。不到几分钟，医生就赶到了，还有两个当地人也参与了抢救。如此这番的表现，应该可以通过护理学校的期末考试。

罗素曾经这样写道：“城市是人类的堕落之所。”但就我在纽约和仰光的经历来看，可以很清楚地看到这两座城市的区别。与人一样，城市也有自己独特的性格。

在什么样的城市，一个急需帮助的陌生人更容易得到帮助？什么样的社会使得市民抑制自己对陌生人的同情？作为一个成熟的社会心理学

systematically exploring these questions.

My students and I have traveled across the United States and much of the world to observe where passersby are most likely to help a stranger. In each city, we have conducted variations on five different field experiments. Our studies have focused on simple acts of assistance as opposed to Schindler-like acts of heroism: Is an "unnoticed" dropped pen retrieved by a passing pedestrian? Does a man with a hurt leg receive assistance picking up a dropped magazine? Will a blind person be helped across a busy intersection? Will a stranger try to make change for a quarter (or its foreign equivalent)? Do people take the time to mail a stamped and addressed "lost" letter?

We've found vast differences between places. In our most recent experiments in 24 U.S. cities, for example, Stephen Reysen and I found the highest helping rates in Knoxville, Tenn. and the lowest in New York City. In earlier experiments conducted in cities in 23 countries, the people of Rio de Janeiro were the most helpful and those in Kuala Lumpur were the lowest (though New York wasn't far behind). The differences were often considerable. In the blind person experiment, for example, five cities (Rio de Janeiro, San Jose, Lilongwe, Madrid and Prague) helped the pedestrian across the street on every occasion, while in Kuala Lampur, Kiev and Bangkok help was offered less than one-half the time. If you have a hurt leg in downtown San Jose (Costa Rica), Calcutta or Shanghai, our results show that you are more than three times as likely to receive help picking up a dropped magazine than if you are on the streets of New York City, Kiev or Sofia. And if you

家，我在过去 20 年中的大多数时间里，都在致力于系统地探索这些问题的答案。

我和我的学生周游美国和全世界大部分地区，去观察哪里的路人最乐意帮助陌生人。在我们到过的每个城市，我们都会做 5 个不同领域的实验的不同变体。我们的研究侧重于一些简单的行善行动，这与辛德勒式的英雄主义相反。比如，一个路人是否会捡起一支扔在地上、不引人注意的钢笔？一个腿脚不方便的人掉了一本杂志后，是否有人会帮他捡起来？是否会有人扶一个盲人走过一个繁忙的十字路口？一个陌生人是否会为了区区 25 美分（或是等值的外国货币）找你零钱？有人会花时间把一封盖上邮戳但没有地址的信送到它该去的地方吗？

我们发现，不同的城市之间结果差异很大。举个例子，在我们最近对美国 24 个城市的调查中，我和斯蒂芬·瑞森发现，帮助比例最高的是田纳西洲的诺克斯维尔，最低的是纽约市。在我们早期实验的 23 个国家的城市中，里约热内卢人最乐意帮助人，而吉隆坡的帮助比率排在最低（尽管纽约也好不了多少）。实验的结果在不同城市之间差异很大。举个例子，在盲人试验中，里约热内卢、圣何塞、利隆圭、马德里和布拉格这五个城市的人，会在任何场合下帮助盲人过马路。但在吉隆坡、基辅和曼谷，两个或许更多的人中才会有一个人愿意帮助陌生人。如果你是个腿脚不便的人，你会发现在圣约瑟（哥斯达黎加首都）、加尔各答或上海的街头，你不小心丢下杂志时，肯帮你捡起杂志的人比在纽约、

drop your pen behind you in New York City, you have less than one-third the chance of seeing it again than if you dropped it in Rio de Janeiro.

Our most important finding, however, is that the helpfulness of a city is systematically related to specific social, economic and demographic characteristics. In our U.S. study, for example, we found that more helpful cities had smaller population sizes, populations densities, more vital economies and slower paces of life.

Last July the first-ever conference on "The Science of Compassion" was held in Telluride, Colo. The notion of studying compassion scientifically may rub some people the wrong way. Is there anything to be gained by reducing humanism to numbers? Our studies indicate there very well might be. By understanding the conditions that bring out the best in people, we may be able to create more compassionate environments.

基辅和索菲亚的大街上要多三倍。还有，如果你在纽约的街头上掉了一支钢笔，你会发现，帮助你的人比在里约热内卢的人少三分之一。

然而，我们最重要的发现是，一个城市的帮助比例是与其社会、经济和人口学特征紧密相连的。举个例子，我们在美国的研究发现，帮助比例越高的城市，其人口规模、人口稠密度越小，经济更有活力，生活节奏也更缓慢。

去年7月，第一次“怜悯的科学”会议在科罗拉多的泰莱瑞德召开。科学地研究怜悯这一课题也许令很多人走了岔路。用数字来计算人道主义有意义吗？我们的研究证明，这也许是非常有价值的。我们也许能凭借理解使人良善的条件，来创造出更多充满怜悯之心的环境。

Authenticity—Why People Aren't Themselves
真实性——为什么你不是你自己

◎ Bella Enahoro

Why should you be yourself? The simple answer is "because everyone else is taken"—it's both the simple answer and an **accurate**① answer. The important question is "why are we not ourselves?" What is the pay off for not being ourselves? Ah, now we're talking.

To begin with, what would cause us to not want to be ourselves? For some of us, we may have been raised in environments where it was dangerous to be who we are. Even as adults we may be working in environments that demand that we be other than who we are in order to ensure job security. So we conclude, I have to be other than I am to get what I want i.e. love, safety, income etc.

We may have learned to believe "who I am is not good enough to be loved, guaranteed safety, approved of". We may have been told "who you are is not worth treating well". We may have learned "who you are is not good

① accurate ['ækjərɪt] adj. 精确的

为什么你应该是你自己？答案很简单，“因为每个人都是他们自己”——这既是个简单的答案，也是正确答案。但关键问题是：“为什么我们都不是我们自己了？”不是我们自己，我们会得到什么好处呢？好，我们现在就来谈谈这个问题。

首先，是什么原因导致我们不想成为我们自己？对于有些人，我们可能在成为自己就会很危险的环境中长大。甚至和我们一起共事的大人们要求我们成为别人而不是自己来确保我们的工作。所以我们断定，未来想得到我们想要的，例如，爱、安全、收入等，我们必须成为别人，而不是自己。

我们也许已经学会相信：“我自己本身不够优秀可以得到爱、获得安全以及被认同。”我们也许被告知：“你不值得好好对待。”我们也可能听到：“你还难以达到我对‘足够好’的标准。”我们也许越加确信自己还不够好，还可以做得更好。

enough to meet my standards for 'being good enough'". We may become convinced that we are less than we should be.

When we feel not good enough what happens to our lives? We end up putting things on hold until we feel we "deserve" by becoming good enough. We spend so much time striving to feel that we're good enough. Have I accomplished enough, am I good looking enough, is my car big/fast/exclusive enough, is my job title high enough, do I have enough awards to be good enough? Exhausting isn't it?

Self worth and **authenticity**① are intrinsically linked. The worth we have in our own eyes, a sense of worth not built on acquisition, job title, appearance, credentials—is the only worth, worth living out of. How many of us realize that we have an intrinsic worth greater than anything on the outside? If we go through life with a sense of being deficient then we are motivated to acquire value—the things that others value in the world then become our aim in life. I may not be good enough in and of myself but look what I've got, becomes our calling card.

Sooner or later, things fall apart, if we're lucky. It can take many forms e.g. we can lose everything we spent our whole lives accruing or we meet someone or a situation who places no value on our "social bling". We run helter skelter trying to get them to "see" us as our bling or we go somewhere else. But there's a crack in the tea cup. When it finally breaks open, our break down becomes our breakthrough.

---

① authenticity [ˌɔθən'tɪsətɪ] n. 真实性，确实性；可靠性

当我们感觉自己不够优秀时，我们的生活会发生什么？我们不再坚持拥有某些东西，直到我们感觉自己已变得更优秀而“值得拥有”的时候。我们花了太多时间去努力感觉自己是否已足够优秀：我是否达到了足够的标准，我是否足够好看，我的车是否够大、够独特、跑得够快，我的职位是否够高，我是否有足够好可以得到足够的奖赏？真是让人感到筋疲力尽啊，有没有？

自我价值和真实性是有本质联系的。价值感不是建立在获得的东西、职称、外貌和文凭上，我们自己眼中的价值是唯一的价值，生活的价值。我们当中有多少人意识到自己有内在价值，这比起一切外在的都要更好？如果我们总是怀着“不足感”度过我们的人生，那么我们会被驱使着去获得价值——世上被人重视的东西会变成你的人生目标。我自己本身也许还不够好，但是看看我已经获得的，它们已成为了我们的名片。

如果我们幸运的话，事物迟早会破碎。它呈现出很多形式，比如，我们会失去花了一辈子追求的东西，或者我们碰到某人或某种境况，他们对我们的“社交着装”不屑一顾。我们慌忙奔跑，试图让他们像看到珠宝一样看到我们，或者我们躲到别的地方去。但是茶杯上有条裂缝，当它最终裂开的时候，我们的破碎也成为了我们突破的转折点。

We begin to look for another way. What we've been looking for is a way to feel good about who we are, under all circumstance. We don't always realize it at first since there's much howling in pain and hanging onto fast disappearing "bling".

The **breakthrough**① cracks us wide open and everything we've been taught is "wrong" with us, all the things we've been taught make us "not good enough" stare us in the face. Excruciating at first but if we stay, refuse to take flight, we can transform. Now begins the re-acquainting ourselves with the "real" us, all of it.

There are many transformation technologies from journaling, meditation, prayer, walking, body work, sound, vibrational healing. We tend to gravitate towards one that works for us. Soon the pain subsides, loses its edge. We don't feel so raw. Our lives may be in shambles around us but we can stand to be alive and increasingly we can stand to be ourselves. We live in a time of infinite help with wonderful teachers who can assist us in moving out of our debris; emotional, psychological and spiritual.

Not being who we are, may be something we picked up at our beginning but was never a part of our being and we need not continue with it.

① breakthrough ['brek,θru] n. 突破；突破性进展

我们开始寻找另一种方法。我们一直在寻找的是，在任何情况下能自我感觉良好的方法。我们不总是一开始就能意识到这一点，因为我们会因破碎和迅速消失的“锦衣珠宝”而痛苦哀号。

突破让我们的裂痕加大，我们曾经被教育的东西都与我们产生冲突，那些让我们觉得“自己不够好”的教育赤裸裸地盯着我们。刚开始我们感到受折磨，但是如果我们能继续留下来而不逃之夭夭，我们就会发生改变。所以，从现在起，重新接受真正的自己，接受自己的全部。

我们有很多转移注意力的方法，比如写日志、深思、祈祷、散步、干体力活、唱歌和震动治疗。我们常常被为我们效力的人所吸引。很快，疼痛感会减弱，变得不再那么强烈。我们不会再感觉那么刺痛。周边的生活也许很混乱，但是我们可以坚持活着，并且越来越能坚持做自己。在我们现在所处的时代，我们可以从良师那儿得到无限的帮助，他们能从情感上、心理和精神上帮助我们走出阴霾。

我们也许会在刚开始时选择不做自己，但这毕竟不是真正的自我，我们不能永远这样。

Learn to Live in the Present Moment

学会活在当下

© Richard Carlson

To a large degree, the measure of our peace of mind is determined by how much we are able to live on the present moment. Irrespective of what happened yesterday or last year, and what may or may not happen tomorrow, the present moment is where you are—always!

Without question, many of us have mastered the neurotic art of spending much of our lives worrying about variety of things—all at once. We allow past problems and future concerns to dominate your present moments, so much so that we end up anxious, frustrated, depressed, and hopeless. On the flip side, we also postpone our gratification, our stated priorities, and our happiness, often convincing ourselves that "someday" will be much better than today.

Unfortunately, the same mental dynamics that tell us to look toward the future will only repeat themselves so that "someday" never actually arrives. John Lennon once said, "Life is what is happening while we are busy making other plans." When we are busy making "other plans", our children are busy

作者简介

理查德·卡尔森（Richard Carlson，1961—2006），美国知名演说家，心理咨询专家，新时代激励大师。曾被《人物》杂志选为“最有魅力的人”，并多次受邀参加各类知名谈话节目。其演说、著作等励志作品风靡全球，著有《别为小事抓狂》系列。

我们内心的平和感，很大程度上取决于我们能有几分精力活在当下。不管曾经发生过什么，将来可能会发生什么，此时此刻才定是最关键的！

毫无疑问，总是将精力放在担心各种各样的事情上，已经成了很多人掌握的一种略微神经质的艺术。我们总是让过去的困扰和未来的担忧控制着现在的生活，以至于我们总是以焦虑、挫败、苦闷和绝望的心情结束思考。另一方面，我们也总是安慰自己“有朝一日”会比今天更好，而对满足感、当下要事、幸福感后知后觉。

可惜，告诉自己“向前看”也仅是被翻来覆去地当作一种精神动力，“有朝一日”总是迟迟不愿现身。约翰·列侬曾说：“生活，就是当我们忙于别的事情时所发生的事。”当我们在“忙别的事”时，我们的孩子

growing up, the people we love are moving away and dying, our bodies are getting out of shape, and our dreams are slipping away. In short, we miss out on life.

Many people lives as if life is a dress rehearsal for some later date. It isn't. In fact, no one has a guarantee that he or she will be here tomorrow. Now is the only time we have, and the only time that we have any control over. When our attention is in the present moment, we push fear from our minds. Fear is the concern over events that might happen in the future—we won't have enough money, our children will get into trouble, we will get old and die whatever.

To combat fear, the best strategy is to learn to bring your attention back to the present. Mark Twain said, "I have been through some terrible things in life, some of which actually happened." I don't think I can say it any better. Practice keeping your attention on the here and now. Your effort will pay great dividends.

正在成长，我们挚爱的人正在离开或死亡，我们的身材正在走样，我们的梦想正在悄悄溜走。简而言之，我们其实错过了生活。

许多人以为生活可以彩排和预演。但其实它不能。实际上，没人能保证他明天依然无恙。“现在”是我们唯一能够拥有和把握的时刻。只有当我们的焦点放在此时此刻，才能排挤掉内心的不安。恐惧是对未来可能发生的事所表现的忧虑——我们缺钱，我们的孩子会遇到麻烦，我们会变老甚至死去……

为了克服恐惧，最好的办法就是将你的注意力拉回到当下。马克·吐温曾说：“我已经克服了那些曾经在生活中真实发生过的困境。”我认为这句话再正确不过了。试着练习集中注意力，活在当下。而你的付出必将获得巨大的回报。

成长在灵魂高处

Reading makes a full man, conference a ready man, and writing an exact man.

——Bacon

阅读使人充实，交谈使人机智，写作使人精确。

——培根

Companionship of Books
以书为伴

◎ Samuel Smiles

A man may usually be known by the books he reads as well as by the company he keeps; for there is a companionship of books as well as of men; and one should always live in the best company, whether it be of books or of men.

A good book may be among the best of friends. It is the same today that it always was, and it will never change. It is the most patient and cheerful of companions. It does not turn its back upon us in times of adversity or distress. It always receives us with the same kindness; amusing and instructing us in youth, and comforting and consoling us in age.

Men often discover their affinity to each other by the mutual love they have for a book just as two persons sometimes discover a friend by the admiration which both entertain for a third. There is an old proverb, "Love me, love my dog." But there is more wisdom in this: "Love me, love my book." The book is a truer and higher bond of union. Men can think, feel, and

作者简介

塞缪尔·斯迈尔斯（Samuel Smiles，1812—1904），英国19世纪伟大的道德学家、著名的社会改革家、散文随笔作家，被称为成功学的开山鼻祖。代表作有《品格的力量》《自己拯救自己》等。

通常，看一个人读什么书，就可以了解他的为人，正如看他和什么人交往，就可以了解他的为人一样；因为有人以书为伴，有人以人为伴；无论是与书还是与人为友，我们都应该以最好的为伴。

一本好书可以成为你最好的朋友。它始终如一，过去如此，现在如此，将来也永不会改变。它是最有耐心、最令人愉悦的伴侣。在我们身陷逆境、遭受痛苦时，它也不会背弃我们。它给予我们一如既往的亲切；年轻时，它陶冶我们的情操，指引我们的道路；年老时，它又给予我们慰藉，勉励我们向前。

人们经常因为喜爱同一本书而结识对方，正如两个人因为敬仰同一个人而结为知己一样。有句古谚说道："爱屋及乌。"但还有另一句更具智慧的名语："爱我及书"。书是更真实而高尚的情谊纽带。人们可以通过共同喜爱的作家沟通思想，交流感情，彼此惺惺相惜。他们与他们喜

sympathize with each other through their favorite author. They live in him together, and he in them.

A good book is often the best urn of a life enshrining the best that life could think out; for the world of a man's life is, for the most part, but the world of his thoughts. Thus the best books are treasuries of good words, the golden thoughts, which, remembered and cherished, become our constant companions and comforters.

Books possess an essence of immortality. They are by far the most lasting products of human effort. Temples and statues decay, but books survive. Time is of no account with great thoughts, which are as fresh today as when they first passed through their author's minds, ages ago. What was then said and thought still speaks to us as vividly as ever from the printed page. The only effect of time has been to sift out the bad products; for nothing in literature can long survive but what is really good.

Books introduce us into the best society; they bring us into the presence of the greatest minds that have ever lived. We hear what they said and did; we see the as if they were really alive; we sympathize with them, enjoy with them, grieve with them; their experience becomes ours, and we feel as if we were in a measure actors with them in the scenes which they describe.

The great and good do not die, even in this world. Embalmed in books, their spirits walk abroad. The book is a living voice. It is an intellect to which on still listens

爱的作家彼此相通，情感相融。

一本好书常常如最精美的宝器，绽放着生命的思想的精华；因为一个人的人生境界，主要就体现在其思想的境界上。因此，最好的书是藏着金玉良言和高贵思想的宝库，这些良言和思想若能铭记于心并多加珍视，就会成为我们忠实的伴侣和永恒的慰藉。

书籍具有不朽的本质。它们是人类努力创造的最持久的成果。寺庙和雕像会腐朽，而书却经久长存。对于伟大的思想来说，时间是无关紧要的，多年前初次闪现于作者脑海的伟大思想，今日依然清晰如故。时间惟一的作用是淘汰低劣的作品；因为只有真正的佳作才能经世长存。

书籍将引领我们与最优秀的人为伍；它使我们与各个时代的伟大智者促膝谈心。如闻其声，如观其行，如见其人；与他们惺惺相惜，悲喜与共，感同身受。我们觉得自己仿佛是一个演员，与他们共同演绎他们所描绘的舞台。

伟大和美好不会逝去，即使是在人世间。他们的精神被载入史册，传于天下。书是人至今仍在聆听的声音，永远充满智慧和活力。

The Joys of Writing
写作的乐趣

◎ Winston Churchill

The fortunate people in the world—the only really fortunate people in the world, in my mind, are those whose work is also their pleasure. The class is not a large one, not nearly so large as it is often represented to be; and authors are perhaps one of the most important elements in its composition. They enjoy in this respect at least a real harmony of life. To my mind, to be able to make your work your pleasure is the one class distinction in the world worth striving for; and I do not wonder that others are inclined to envy those happy human beings who find their livelihood in the gay effusions of their fancy, to whom every hour of labour is an hour of enjoyment, to whom repose—however necessary—is a tiresome interlude. And even a holiday is almost deprivation. Whether a man writes well or ill, has much to say or little, if he cares about writing at all, he will appreciate the pleasures of composition. To sit at one's table on a sunny morning, with four clear hours of uninterruptible security, plenty of nice white paper, and a squeezer pen—that is true happiness. The

作者简介

温斯顿·丘吉尔（Winston Churchill，1874—1965），政治家、画家、演说家、作家以及记者。1953 年因作品《不需要战争》获诺贝尔文学奖，曾两度任英国首相。被美国杂志《展示》列为近百年来世界最有说服力的八大演说家之一，2002 年获得 BBC“有史以来最伟大的英国人”称号。

在我看来，世界上幸运的人——世界上唯一真正幸运的人，是那些干着自己喜爱工作的人。这类人并不多，比幸运这个词平常所代表的数量少太多；而作家也许是组成这类人最重要的部分之一。在这一方面，他们至少享受着生活中真正的和谐。依我看，让工作成为一种乐趣，是世界上值得追求的一类荣誉。而我从不怀疑有人会嫉妒这些幸福者，他们在他们奇特构思的快乐源泉中找到了谋生之道，对这些人来说，每个小时的劳动都是一个小时的享受，而休息——无论多么必要——都是无聊的幕间表演。甚至度假也是一种乐趣被剥夺的感觉。一个人写得是好是坏，想说的是多是少，只要真心喜欢写作，就会享受到创作带来的乐趣。在一个阳光明媚的清晨，坐在书桌前，伴着整整不被打扰的四个小时，一摞赏心的雪白稿纸，外加一支挤压式钢笔——这就是真正的幸福。

complete absorption of the mind upon an agreeable occupation—what more is there than that to desire? What does it matter what happens outside? The House of Commons may do what it likes, and so may the House of Lords. The heathen may rage furiously in every part of the globe. The bottom may be knocked clean out of the American market. Consols may fall and suffragettes may rise. Nevermind, for four hours, at any rate, we will withdraw ourselves from a common, ill-governed, and disorderly world, and with the key of fancy unlock that cupboard where all the good things of the infinite are put away.

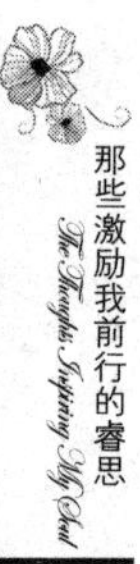

全身心专注于一种令人愉快的职业——此外还有何可求呢？外面发生天大的事又有什么打紧？下议院爱干什么干什么去，上议院也一样。异教徒可以遍布全世界各个角落，美国市场尽可翻个底朝天，公债也可尽情涨跌，女权运动也可随意翻腾。都无所谓，无论如何，在这四个小时里，我们可以将自己拖离这个粗俗、放纵、混乱的世界，用想象力这把钥匙，去开启收藏了宇宙中所有美好事物的柜橱。

How to Talk to Anyone, Anytime, Anywhere
谈话的艺术

◎ Larry King

I never wanted to be anything but a broadcaster, a talker. And for 40 years, I've been doing just that. To me, the ability to talk well is one of the great pleasures in life and can bring with it some of life's greatest rewards.

I'm not saying it's always easy. The vast majority of people would rather jump out of an airplane without a parachute than sit next to someone they've never met at a dinner party.

But the more you work at it, the easier it will be. To get you started, here are my six basic ingredients for learning how to talk to anyone, anytime, anywhere.

1. You Don't Have to Be Quotable

If you could have witnessed my first morning in broadcasting, you would have bet the ranch that I was the last guy who'd survive, much less succeed, as a professional talker.

It happened at WAER, a small radio station in Miami Beach, on the

作者简介

拉里·金（Larry King，1933— ），美国著名主持人，有“世界最富盛名的王牌主持人”之称。曾获艾美奖，写过多本书籍，被《时代》杂志称为“麦克风霸主”。他主持的“拉里·金现场”是美国有线新闻网（CNN）收视率最高的节目；2012年2月，拉里·金正式结束CNN任职。

我从来没有想过从事别的工作，除了当一名电视台主播，做一个谈话者。40年来，我一直都在做这份工作。对我来说，侃侃而谈的能力可以带来巨大的生活乐趣，也可以带来人生中一些最好的回报。

我并不是说这份工作总是很容易。绝大多数人宁愿不带降落伞跳下飞机，也不愿在宴会上坐在从未谋面的陌生人旁边。

但是，你练习得越多，与人谈话就会变得越容易。在你开始学习如何跟任何人在任何时间地点谈话之前，请看我列出的以下六个基本要点。

1. 你不必字字珠玑

如果你见过我首次播报早间新闻的情景，你肯定会打赌我很难在职业生涯中走下去，更别说做一个专业的谈话者了。

那是1957年5月1日的时候，在迈阿密海滩的一个小电台WAER。

morning of May 1, 1957. I had been hanging around there hoping to crash into my dream world of radio. The station's general manager liked my voice but didn't have any openings.

I lived near the station and went by every day, watching the disc jockeys, the newscasters, the sports announcers. After three weeks the morning deejay quit. The manager told me I had the job starting Monday morning.

I didn't sleep that whole weekend. I kept **rehearsing**[①] things to say. By Monday I was a basket case.

The manager called me into his office to wish me luck. And then I was on the air.

Picture me at 9 a.m. sitting in the studio with my new theme song, Les Elgart's "Swinging Down the Lane" cued up. I start the song. Then I fade the music down so I can talk. Only nothing comes out. My mouth feels like cotton.

So I bring the music up and fade it again. Still no words coming out of my mouth. It happens a third time. The only thing my listeners are hearing is a record going up and down in volume.

Finally, the **exasperated**[②] manage kicks open the door to the control room and shouts, "This is a communications business!" Then he turns and leaves, slamming the door behind him.

In that instant, I leaned toward the microphone and said: "Good morning.

---

① rehearse [ri'hə:s] v. 预演，排演；预先演习；详述；复述

② exasperated [ig'zæspəreitid] adj. 恼怒的

当时我一直在那里无所事事地闲逛，希望借此开启我所梦想的广播世界。电台的总经理喜欢我的声音，但那时台里没有空缺职位。

我住的地方离电台很近。于是我每天都会过去，看音乐节目主持人、新闻主播、体育新闻播音员在那里工作。三个星期后，早间时段的音乐节目主持人辞职了，经理便让我星期一上午开始上班。

我整个周末都没睡，一直在排练要说的东西。到周一的时候，我几乎快精神崩溃了。

经理把我叫进他的办公室，给了我祝福。然后我就开始了第一次播音。

你可以想象一下，上午 9 点，我坐在工作室里，旁边放着新的主题歌曲——莱斯・埃尔加特的《一路摇摆》。我开始播放这首歌。然后我把音乐的音量降下来，开始说话。但我什么也没说出来，我的嘴就像棉花一样绵软无力。

于是我把音乐声音调大，之后又调小。但我的嘴里仍没能吐出一个词来。第三次尝试还是一样的结果。我的听众听到的只是音乐的音量上上下下调个不停。

最后，气急败坏的经理踢开控制室的门，高声叫道："这是一个交谈的活计！"然后他转身离去，猛地把身后的门"砰"地一声关上了。

This is my first day on the radio. I've been practicing all weekend. But my mouth is dry. I'm nervous. The general manager just kicked open the door and said, 'This is a communication business.'" I wasn't exactly quotable that morning, but I was able to get some thing out by telling my listeners about the **predicament**① I was in, and that gave me the confidence to continue. The rest of the show—as well as my career—went fine.

2. Attitude Counts

After that fiasco in Miami, I made a commitment to keep talking even when it might not be comfortable—in other words, to work at it. The right attitude—the will to talk—is crucial to becoming a better talker.

I think one reason I've had a certain amount of success in broadcasting is that the audience can see I love what I'm doing. You can't fake that. And if you try, you will fail.

Tommy Lasorda, the former manager of the Los Angeles Dodgers, once came on my radio show the night after his team suffered a crushing loss in the National League playoffs. From his enthusiasm you never would have guessed he was the losing manager.

When I asked him how he could be so **exuberant**②, he said, "The best day of my life is when I manage a winning game. The second-best day of my life is when I manage a losing game." That enthusiasm and his willingness to

---

① predicament [pri'dikəmənt] n. 困境

② exuberant [ig'zju:bərənt] adj. 兴高采烈的；繁茂的；丰富的

在那一瞬间，我前倾着身体，对着麦克风说："早上好。这是我第一天做广播节目。我整个周末都一直在练习，练得嘴巴很干。我很紧张。总经理刚刚又踢门进来说，'这是一个交谈的活计'。"那天早上我所说的并没什么值得引用的话，但我能够讲出一些东西，把我的困境告诉听众。这给了我继续做下去的信心。那天剩下的节目时间——以及我后来的职业生涯——进展得都还不错。

2. 态度很重要

经过迈阿密的惨败之后，我下定决心：即使在不舒服的情况下，我也要不停地讲话——换句话说，不断努力练习。正确的态度——谈话的意愿——这是至关重要的，只有这样，你才能成为一个更好的谈话者。

我想，我能在广播上取得一定的成功，原因之一就是观众可以看出我对自己工作的热爱。这是无法伪装出来的。如果你只是尽力伪装，那你必将失败。

汤米·莱索达，前洛杉矶道奇队的经理，当他的球队在国联季后赛中遭受毁灭性的惨败后，第二天晚上，他就出现在我的广播节目里。从与他谈话的热情里，你绝对不会想到他的球队刚刚遭到惨败。

当我问他为何可以如此精力旺盛时，他说："我人生中最好的一天就是我管理的球队成功赢得比赛的时候。第二好的一天就是我管理的球队

share it have made him a successful manager and a very successful talker too.

3. Remember to Take Turns

Careful listening makes you a better talker. Good follow-up questions are the mark of a good conversationalist. In fact, I have an important rule that I remind myself every morning: nothing I say this day will teach me anything; so if I'm going to learn, I have to do it by listening.

4. Broaden Your Horizons

The best conversationalists are able to talk about issues and experiences beyond their own daily lives. You can expand your world through travel, but you can also do it without leaving your own backyard.

When I was a boy, my widowed mother got an elderly woman to care for us while Mom tried to scrape up money for food, clothing and to keep our little apartment. The helper's father had fought in the Civil War, and as a child she had actually seen Abraham Lincoln. I was able to talk to her, so in a way my childhood was a window on another era in history.

The point is this: people with backgrounds different from your own can help broaden your conversational **repertoire**① and your thinking.

5. Keep It Light

One of my cardinal rules of conversation is never stay too serious too

---

① repertoire ['repətwɑ:] n. 全部节目；全部才能

输掉比赛的时候。”这种热情与分享精神已经使他成为一个成功的经理，也成了一个非常成功的谈话者。

3. **记得努力倾听**

仔细倾听他人的声音能让你成为更好的交谈者。不断提出好问题是一个优秀谈话者的标志。事实上，我每天早上都提醒自己要注意一条重要规则：我说的东西对自己毫无教益，所以如果我要学习，我就必须努力倾听。

4. **开阔你的视野**

最好的谈话者能够谈论超出自己日常生活范围的问题和经历。你可以通过旅行来扩展你的视野，但你也可以足不出户就丰富自己的阅历。

当我还是个小男孩时，我那守寡的母亲委托一位老奶奶照顾我们，而她自己则在外面努力工作赚钱，以供我们饮食穿衣，支付我们小公寓的租金。老奶奶的父亲曾参加过国内战争。当时她还只是一个孩子，但她亲眼见过亚伯拉罕·林肯。我可以跟她交谈，所以在某种程度上，我的童年为我打开了通往另一个历史时代的窗口。

我认为，与自己背景不同的人能帮助扩展你的交谈能力，让你的思想更开阔、更深刻。

5. **保持轻松愉快的氛围**

我谈话的一个基本规则就是永远不要太久地保持严肃氛围。同样，

long. Similarly, a key quality I look for in a potential guest is a sense of humor, preferably self-deprecating. Frank Sinatra is one guest who's never been afraid to make fun of himself.

During an interview with me, Sinatra recalled comedian Don Rickles coming over to his table at a Las Vegas restaurant to ask a favor. Rickles was dining with a friend.

"Would you mind saying hi to her, Frank?"

"Of course not," the singer replied. "Bring her over."

Then Rickles said that his friend would be even more impressed if Sinatra could come over to their table. So a short time later, Sinatra good-naturedly walked across the restaurant, slapped Rickles on the back and said how delighted he was to see him.

Whereupon Rickles said, "Beat it, Frank. This is personal."

What's key to the story—and most appealing to the audience—is that Sinatra so obviously enjoys retelling this joke at his own expense.

6. Be the Genuine You

Anybody I've ever talked to for more than a few minutes knows at least two things about me: I'm from Brooklyn, New York, and I'm Jewish. That's because I'm deeply proud of both.

You should be as open and honest with your conversational partners as you'd want them to be with you, willing to reveal what your background is and what your likes and dislikes are. That's part of the give-and-take of

我想从潜在嘉宾身上找到的关键品质就是幽默感，而且最好有自嘲精神。弗兰克·辛纳特拉就是一位从不害怕取笑自己的嘉宾。

在一次采访中，辛纳特拉回忆起喜剧演员唐·瑞克斯曾在拉斯维加斯的餐馆里请求他帮忙的事。当时，瑞克斯正在和朋友吃饭。

“你能过去和我朋友打声招呼吗，弗兰克？”

“当然可以，”辛纳特拉说，“把她叫过来吧。”

然后，瑞克斯说道，如果辛纳特拉能到他们的餐桌来，那他的朋友一定会更满意。所以，过了一会儿，辛纳特拉满怀善意地穿过餐厅，轻轻拍了拍瑞克斯的背，并跟他说很高兴见到他。

于是瑞克斯对他说道：“走开，弗兰克。注意这是私人场合。”

这个故事的关键——最吸引观众的就是——辛纳特拉显然很喜欢重复讲述这个故事，自己取笑自己。

6. 做真实的自己

和我交谈过几分钟的人都知道与我有关的至少两件事：我来自纽约布鲁克林，以及我是犹太人。因为我为这两者而感到无比骄傲。

如果你希望你的谈话对象能对你开诚布公，那你就应该对他们敞开心扉，真诚沟通，愿意透露你的背景，分享你喜欢的和不喜欢的东西。这样，你才能在谈话时保持分享和获取信息之间的平衡，才能不断地了

conversation, part of getting to know people.

Talk-show hosts Regis Philbin and Kathie Lee Gifford come into our homes easily and naturally, and they're not afraid to reveal their tastes or tell stories on themselves. Without making themselves the focus of their talk, they are themselves. If they—or a guest—tell a sad or joyful story, they are not afraid to show their feelings.

Mel Tillis, the successful country-and-western singer, is absolutely charming as an interview guest, even though he stutters. It doesn't show up when he's singing, but it does when he's talking. Instead of letting it bother him, Mel is upfront about the problem, jokes about it, and is so completely at ease with himself that he puts you at ease too.

As for myself, I learned something critical after surviving that case of "mike fright" on my first day of broadcasting: be honest, and you won't go wrong.

Whether you're talking to one person or a million, the rules are the same. It's all about making a connection. Show empathy, enthusiasm and a willingness to listen, and you can't help becoming a master of talk.

解他人。

脱口秀主持人里吉斯・菲尔宾和凯西・李・吉福德会很轻松自然地来到我家，他们并不害怕暴露他们的品味，或者讲述自己身上发生的故事。他们在谈话时，并不会刻意让自己成为焦点，而是表现出真实的自己。如果他们——或者一位客人——讲了一个悲伤或快乐的故事，他们并不害怕流露出自己的情感。

梅尔・蒂利什，一位成功的乡村音乐歌手，绝对是一个魅力十足的采访嘉宾，尽管他说话有些口吃。他唱歌时并不结巴，但他说话时确实会口齿不太利索。他没有因为口吃而深受困扰，反而勇敢地面对这个问题，还拿它开玩笑，在完全放松的状态下自得其乐，让你也倍感轻松愉快。

至于我自己，在头一天广播时经历了“麦克风恐惧症”并幸存下来后，我学到了关键的一点：要诚实，你就不会出错。

不论你现在是跟一个人或一百万人谈话，规则是不变的。交谈实质上就是要与他人建立一种联系。时刻保持对话的热情，总是愿意理解他人、倾听他人，那你自然而然便会成为谈话大师。

My Declaration of Self-esteem
我的成长宣言

© Virginia Satir

The following was written in answer to a 15-year-old girl's question, "How can I prepare myself for a fulfilling life?"

I am me.

In all the world, there is no one else exactly like me. There are persons who have some parts like me, but no one adds up exactly like me. Therefore, everything that comes out of me is authentically mine because I alone choose.

I own everything about me—my body, including everything it does; my mind, including all its thoughts and ideas; my eyes, including the images of all they behold; my feelings, whatever they may be—anger, joy, frustration, love, disappointment, excitement; my mouth, and all the words that come out of it, polite, sweet or rough, correct or incorrect; my voice, loud or soft; and all my actions, whether they be to others or to myself.

I own my fantasies, my dreams, my hopes, my fears.

I own all my triumphs and successes, all my failures and mistakes.

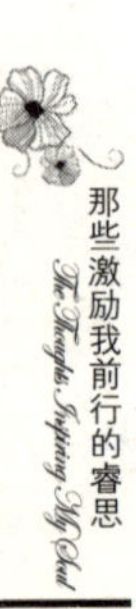

作者简介

维吉尼亚·萨提亚（Virginia Satir，1916—1988），美国著名心理治疗师、家庭治疗师。她是第一代的家庭治疗师，从50年代起已居于领导地位。代表作有《萨提亚治疗实录》《新家庭如何塑造人》等。

一个15岁女孩曾向我提出问题："我该怎么做，才能过一个充实的生活？"以下就是我的答案。

做你自己。

在这个世界上，没有任何一个人和我一样。有些人可能与我有某些相似之处，但没有人同我一模一样。所以，我的一切都有我独一无二的特性，因为这是我自己的选择。

我是我自己的主人——我的身体，包括所有的一切；我的头脑，包括所有的想法思绪；我的眼睛，包括所看到的一切景象；我的感觉，不论是生气还是喜悦，失望沮丧还是兴奋快乐；我的嘴巴，我所说的一字一句，无论是中听还是逆耳，无论是对还是错；我的声音，不管是嘹亮还是轻柔；以及我的所有行为，不管是对他人还是对自己的一举一动。

我有我的幻想，我的美梦，我的希望，我的恐惧。

胜利和成功由我自己创造，失败和错误由我自己承担。

Because I own all of me, I can become intimately acquainted with me. By so doing I can love me and be friendly with me in all my parts. I can then make it possible for all of me to work in my best interests.

I know there are aspects about myself that puzzle me, and other aspects that I do not know. But as long as I am friendly and loving to myself, I can courageously and hopefully look for the solutions to the puzzles and for ways to find out more about me.

However I look and sound, whatever I say and do, and whatever I think and feel at a given moment in time is me. This is authentic and represents where I am at that moment in time. When I review later how I looked and sounded, what I said and did, and how I thought and felt, some parts may turn out to be unfitting. I can discard that which is unfitting and keep that which proved fitting, and invent something new for that which I have discarded.

I can see, hear, feel, think, say, and do. I have the tools to survive, to be close to others, to be productive, and to make sense and order out of the world of people and things outside of me.

I own me, and therefore I can engineer me.

I am me and I am okay.

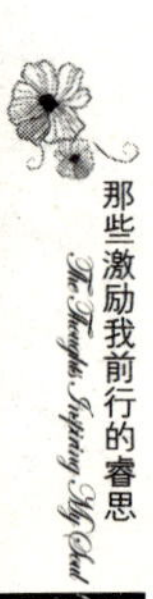

因为我主宰着全部的自己，我深刻地了解自己。所以，我喜欢自己，接纳自己的一切。然后，我能够展现出自己最好的一面。

然而，我知道多少会有些地方让自己困惑，总有一块连自己也无法理解的角落。但是，只要我多多关爱自己，我就可以鼓起勇气和希望，为心中的疑问找到答案，并了解自己更多。

我的所见所闻，我的一言一行，我的所思所想，我都会接受，因为这就是我。这代表了那个时刻最真实的我。而后，当我回顾我的这些一举一动时，会发现有些可能不合时宜。我会摒弃那些不宜之处，保留那些可取之处，并为我之所弃填补新的内容。

我身心健全，而且自力更生。我有生存的技能，我关怀他人，为创造一个更美好的世界而作出贡献。

我拥有自己，因此我会做自己的主宰。

我就是我，我很好。

Dreaming Big
远大梦想

◎ Richard Macalintal

When we were a child and someone asks us a question of what we want when we grow up, we can easily answer and say like "I want to be a doctor" or "I want to be a lawyer".

But now, ask someone in your office what they want in life. Maybe they'll just say they want a phone, they want a car, a new dress or house perhaps.

Dreaming is free but a kid and a grown-up like me have different point of view regarding it. When kids answer to this question, they won't hesitate to answer no matter how big their dreams are. They didn't mean to worry if it's achievable or not. What they do know is that they want it and it can be achieved. It's something that for them, nothing can **hinder**[1] towards realizing it. But as we grow up, we tend to realize that the world is harsh. Given the opportunity to answer the same question, we may pause for a while and think

① hinder ['hɪndə] vt. 阻碍；打扰

当我们还是小孩时，别人问我们长大了想当什么，我们很容易就给出答案，说出“我想当医生”或“我想当律师”这类的话。

但是现在，问你办公室里的人们，他们在生活中想要什么。他们也许只会说想要手机、汽车、新衣服或房子。

梦想是自由的，但是小孩对待梦想的看法和像我这样的成人却有所不同。当小孩回答这个问题时，无论他们的梦想有多大，他们都会毫不犹豫。他们不会担心梦想是否会实现。他们真正清楚的是他们想得到它并且会实现。似乎对他们来说，任何事都阻挡不了他们去实现梦想。然而对于我们成年人，我们逐渐意识到世界的残酷性。当我们有机会回答同样的问题时，我们会停顿一会儿，然后想些现实的、且更容易做到的事。简言之，我们的梦想会更小。这主要的原因是我们的心态被众多现实所影响，因而我们害怕有大梦想。我们倾向分析很多从而限制了我们考虑大梦想的能力。最终，这种害怕成为我们追求更好生活的障碍。

of something that can be realistic and more **achievable**[1]. In short, we might dream something smaller. This is mainly because our mindset is affected by lots of facts that give us fear of dreaming big. We tend to analyze a lot thus limiting our ability to think big. As a result, this fear becomes a hindrance to achieve greater things in life.

More importantly, are we really living the dream we set out to dream? Was our dream big enough? Did we even have a dream? It turns out that one of the main reasons we work really hard without getting very far is because we don't have an inspiring long term **vision** that leads us, step-by-step, into the future of our dreams. Most of the time, we've either forgotten our dreams or didn't have one to start out with. As Victor Hugo said, "There is nothing like a dream to create the future." We need a dream, and we need to dream big! In business terminology, the dream is typically called the Vision, and it defines the final destination of your business success. The dream tells you where you are going and becomes, in effect, your North Star.

So start dreaming big, opportunities are endless!

① achievable [ə'tʃivəbl] adj. 可完成的；可有成就的；做得到的

更重要的是，我们确实实现了我们打算实现的梦想了吗？我们的梦想足够大吗？我们是否还有梦想呢？结果表明，我们努力工作却没有很大的进步，其主要原因之一就是我们没有一个长远且激励人心的目标，来指引我们一步步地走向梦想中的未来。大多数的时间里，我们要么忘记了自己的梦想，要么就没有梦想。正如维克特·雨果所说："创造未来的只有梦想。"我们需要梦想，我们需要远大的梦想！在商业术语中，梦想被典型地称为愿景，表示商业成功的最终目标。梦想告诉你该往哪走，你要成为什么，事实上，它就是指引你的北极星。

所以梦想远大，机会无限！

Motivation Does Wonders

动力造就奇迹

◎ Ammarah Khan

If going through the pages of history, you will find dozens of such failures who replaced their defeat by taking successive attempts. This is noticeable that success is never at your door step, this is your attitude towards your destination and your continuous hard work that it brings there. On the other side, daily papers illustrate ample of such examples of individuals who embrace suicide because they lose heart at the cries of unsuccessful results. What is the difference between these two cases, this is the presence of eminent force of motivation in former's life which unfortunately may be absent in the later ones'.

Though motivation does not have any **substantial**[①] existence, yet it generates and springs out such results which change the entire life of an individual or community. While criticizing, we often forget that there are already numbers of despairing factors in our society which prevail to discourage an individual's efforts. We ignore that by commenting on someone's honest hard work, in fact we are degrading human grace. Many of our kids suffer and go in deep inferiority complex just because there is no one

① substantial [səb'stænʃ(ə)l] adj. 大量的；实质的；内容充实的

如果你翻看历史，你会发现很多失败者都会化悲愤为力量，失败之后会不断地努力。显而易见，成功从来都不是信手拈来的，它取决于你对待目标的态度和坚持不懈的努力。另一方面，日报刊登了大量因失败灰心而自杀的案例。这两者之间的不同在于，前者的生命存在着强大的动力，不幸的是，后者没有。

虽然动力不是客观存在的东西，但是它可以产生改变整个个人生活或社会的结果。在我们进行批判的时候，我们常常忘了社会中已经存在大量令人绝望的因素，而这些因素普遍会阻拦人们的努力。我们通过对别人的努力程度的评判而忽视它，但事实上，我们在贬低人性魅力。我们的许多孩子仅仅因为没有人激励他们，甚至没有获得一丁点儿的称赞，从而遭受并陷入深深的自卑感当中。

to motivate them; there is not even a single bit of appreciation for them.

Mostly people are very much sure about their future targets but are confused about what should they choose and what is exactly as per their nature. For this case motivation is very much **beneficial**[1] as it encourages you to reach your ambition. It helps you to develop confidence in your abilities and encourages you to step ahead without getting worried how hard your target may be. Therefore, to have some motivational hand behind you is much important.

Motivation does wonders, it will help you to make strategic plans to overcome hurdles smoothly and reach the target efficiently. It serves you to discover the hurdles and challenges that might come in your way and gives you courage to cope with them. You will be encouraged by your internal spirit to find errors and lacking in them that are becoming hurdles to meet you goals.

Motivation plays a refreshing role. It suggests ways to bring changes in you and your team especially in the case when you have failed in a certain target and you are feeling depressed and are hearted. You will also get help about how to overcome your errors and to make powerful and adequate abilities so that you become capable of producing maximum in the appropriate field and can get a fruitful result.

If you have someone's motivation behind you, you will definitely get it no matter how hard is the way. Your aim assists you to enhance your potential so that you can give your maximum while working. Your strong self

① beneficial [benɪ'fɪʃ(ə)l] adj. 有益的；有利的；可享利益的

大多数人很明确自己的未来目标，但是他们对自己应该做什么选择感到迷惑，他们不清楚自己的本性到底是怎样的。在这种情况下，动机会激励你追求志向，这时它就显得非常有帮助。它会帮助你提高自己的能力、自信心，激励你无需担心目标有多难，只管大胆迈步向前走。因此，在你身后有个推动力非常重要。

动力造就奇迹，它有助于你制定战略计划，顺利地克服障碍，有效地达到目标。它有益于你发现追求目标的道路上可能出现的障碍和挑战，赐予你勇气去克服它们。你会被你的内心精神激励着发现错误，缺少它们将会成为你达成目标的障碍。

动力起着重振雄心的作用。尤其当你和你的团队在某个目标中失败后感到绝望和心碎之时，它会给你们指引方向，带来改变。你也会在如何克服错误、锻炼强大且足够的能力方面得到帮助。因此，你会在合适的领域有足够的才能发挥最大效率，获得大丰收。

如果你身后有一股推动力，那么无论你的路有多艰苦，你就一定会成功。你的目标有助于你发掘潜能，这样你就可以在工作的时候发挥最

commitments suggest you ways to follow such strategies that would help you to boost up your efforts. It will help you to hone your abilities so that you can perform the best while working or leading a team.

Motivation basically helps a person to attain his ambitions by utilizing all of his internal spirits. It provides motivation for accomplishment of one's ambitions, life work counseling, personality making and other sort of counseling. If you are lucky to get such motivation, you will see that it will work to set targets, affirmative individual development mentoring and other kinds of counseling.

It helps you to reach at your target through beating all the challenges. It suggests strategies and new ways to boost up your competency. It provides turning point of your career. It gives ways how to deal effectively with the clashes on your way to your aim. It helps you to improve your governing and decision making abilities. It helps you to boost up your performance efficiencies. It also suggests solutions and strategies to get out of problems. It helps you to develop leadership qualities in your personality. It also improves self management skills. It suggests you how to deal efficiently with your competitors. It directs how to make team work efficient.

Therefore motivation is very important in individual's life as it gives solution to all the **hurdles**① and complications while establishing or running any career. So, one must establish one must have some motivational spirit to get one's targets in life.

---

① hurdle ['hɜːd(ə)l] n. 障碍；栏；跳栏

大效率。你强烈的自我承诺向你表明，遵从这种战略会帮助你更加努力。它会帮助你锻炼自己的能力，这样，在你工作或领导团队的时候就可以表现得最好。

根本上，动力会帮助人们通过利用个人所有的内在精神来实现志向。这种内在精神会提供动力实现人生志向、计划毕生事业、塑造个人性格和提供建议的能力。如果你足够幸运拥有这个动力，那么你将发现它有利于有效地设定目标、积极的个人发展指导以及提供其他建议。

动力有助于你通过应对挑战达到自己的目标。它将提供策略和新方法来提升你的能力。它会给你的事业带来转折点。它会提供给你有效地处理在实现目标的过程中出现的碰撞。它将帮助你提高自己的管理和决策能力。它将帮助你提高自己的执行效率。它还会为你提供解决问题的办法和对策。它会帮助你发扬你个性中的领导特质。它还会改善自我管理技能。它会教你有效地处理与竞争者的关系。它会指导你如何更有效地进行团队工作。

因此，动力在人的生活中有着极其重要的作用。因为在你建立和发展事业的过程中，它会提供你遇到的所有障碍及复杂问题的解决方法。所以，人必须要拥有动力精神来实现自己的生活目标。

A Letter From Kai-fu Li
李开复致女儿的一封信

Dear Daughter,

As we drove off from Columbia, I wanted to write a letter to you to tell you all that is on my mind.

First, I want to tell you how proud we are. Getting into Columbia is a real **testament**[①] to what a great well-rounded student you are. Your academic, artistic, and social skills have truly blossomed in the last few years. Whether it is getting the highest grade in Calculus, completing your elegant fashion design, successfully selling your painted running shoes, or becoming one of the top orators in Model United Nations, you have become a talented and accomplished young woman. You should be as proud of yourself as we are.

College will be the most important years in your life. It is in college that you will truly discover what learning is about. You often question "what good is this course". I encourage you to be inquisitive, but I also want to tell you: "Education is what you have left after all that is taught is forgotten." What I mean by that is the materials taught isn't as important as you gaining the ability to learn a new subject and the ability to analyze a new problem.

① testament ['tɛstəmənt] n. 遗嘱；证明，证据；信仰声明，自白

亲爱的女儿：

当我们驱车驶离哥伦比亚大学时，我很想提笔写封信给你，把此刻我脑海中的万千思绪转达于你。

首先，我想告诉你，我们为你无比自豪。进入哥伦比亚大学足以证明你是一个如此全面而优异的学生。近几年里，无论你的学业表现，还是你的艺术才能以及社交能力都日臻卓然。你考取过微积分第一名，亲手设计出优雅的时装，成功贩售了自己手绘的跑鞋，甚至你还站上“模拟联合国”的演讲台进行了一次成功的讲演。你已然出落成有才华、有造诣的年轻女性，你同样应该为自己感到自豪。

大学将是你人生中最重要的时光。只有在大学阶段你才会发现学习的真谛。你总喜欢问“这门功课有什么用”。我鼓励你勤思好问，但我同样想告诉你：“教育的实质就是忘光所学之后还能留下的东西。”意即书本上学到的知识并不是最主要的，掌握学习新知的能力和分析新问题的本领才至关重要。这才是大学学习的要义所在——由老师为中心的填鸭式教学变成学生为主的启发式教育，经历这一阶段后你将成为一名自

That is really what learning in college is about—this will be the period where you go from teacher-taught to master-inspired, after which you must become self-learner. So do take each subject seriously, and even if what you learn isn't critical to your life, the skills of learning will be something you cherish forever.

Do not fall into the trap of **dogma**①. There is no single simple answer to any question. Remember during your high school debate class, I always asked you to take on the side that you don't believe in? I did that for a reason—things are rarely "black and white", and there are always many ways to look at a problem. You will become a better problem solver if you recognize that. This is called "critical thinking", and it is the most important thinking skill you need for your life. This also means you need to become tolerant and supportive of others. I will always remember when I went to my Ph.D. advisor and proposed a new thesis topic. He said "I don't agree with you, but I'll support you." After the years, I have learned this isn't just flexibility, it is encouragement of critical thinking, and an **empowering**② style of leadership, and it has become a part of me. I hope it will become a part of you too.

Follow your passion in college. Take courses you think you will enjoy. Don't be trapped in what others think or say. Steve Jobs says when you are in college, your passion will create many dots, and later in your life you will connect them. In his great speech given at Stanford's commencement,

① dogma ['dɔgmə] n. 教义，信条；武断的意见，教条
② empower [ɛm'paʊɚ] v. 授权，使有权；许可，使能够

主的学习者。所以，即使所学看似无关紧要，也应认真对待每门功课，从中悟到的学习技能将会令你受用终生。

凡事不要武断，任何问题都不会简单到只有一个答案。还记得你高中时的辩论课么，我总是让你站到你否认的那一方来论辩。我之所以这么做是因为，事情很少是非黑即白的，而且一个问题常常可以换多个角度来看。如果能意识到这一点，你将会在面对问题时游刃有余。这叫做“批判性思维”，是你人生中最需要的一种思考能力，意味着你要包容和接纳不同于你的他人观点。我永远记得，在读博士时我曾向我的导师提出一个新论题，他对我说：“我不同意你，但我支持你。”多年后，我认识到这不仅仅是一种变通的说辞，更是一种对批判性思考的鼓励，一种敢于放手的领导作风，这一点已经融入我的处事之道，我希望这也能成为你的人生哲学。

在大学里，要追随自己的热情之所在。选择自己喜欢的课程。不要被他人的想法或意见所左右。史蒂夫·乔布斯曾说过，读大学时你的热情会创建出许多个兴趣点，而在日后的人生中这些点将被一个个串连起来。在他为斯坦福大学毕业典礼所做的著名演说中，他举了自身这样一

he gave the great example where he took calligraphy, and a decade later, it became the basis of the beautiful Macintosh fonts, which later ignited desktop publishing and brought wonderful tools like Microsoft Word to our lives. His expedition into calligraphy was a dot, and Macintosh became the connecting line. So don't worry too much about what job you will have, and don't be too **utilitarian**①, and if you like Japanese or Korean, go for it, even if your dad thinks "it's not useful". Enjoy picking your dots, and be assured one day you will find your calling, and connect a beautiful curve through the dots.

Do your best in classes, but don't let pressure get to you. Your mother and I have no expectations for your grades. If you graduate and learn something in your four years, we would feel happy. Your Columbia degree will take you far, even if you don't graduate with honors. So please don't give yourself pressure. During your last few months in high school, you were so happy because there was little pressure and college applications are finished. But in the past few weeks, we saw you are beginning to worry (did you know you bite your nails when you are nervous?). Please don't be worried. The only thing that matters is that you learned. The only metric you should use is that you tried. Grades are just silly letters that give the vain people something to brag, and the lazy people something to fear. You are too good to be either.

Most importantly, make friends and be happy. College friends are often the best in life, because during college you are closer to them physically than to your family. Also, going through independence and adulthood is a natural

---

① utilitarian [ju,tɪlɪ'tɛriən] adj. 有效用的，实用的；功利主义的

个很好的例子：他在大学里凭着兴趣修学了书法，而十年后，这成了建立苹果机漂亮字体库的基础，并由此生发出了后来的桌面出版系统，也使得像微软文档这样的出色软件得以走进我们的生活。应该说，对书法艺术的探索就是他人生中的一个点，而苹果机的出现则是连起这个点的那条线。所以不必太担心你将来要从事什么工作，也不要有太强的功利心。如果你喜欢日语或者韩语，就去学吧，哪怕爸爸认为“那没用”。尽情选择你人生的兴趣点吧，并坚信有一天你会在其间找到自己职业生涯的契机，藉由这些点勾勒出生命中一道优美的曲线。

课业上要努力，但不要给自己太多压力。你母亲和我在成绩上对你没有过多要求，只要你顺利毕业并在四年里有所学得，我们就很高兴了。即便你没能以优异的成绩毕业，哥伦比亚大学这一起点也足以让你行得更远。所以千万别给自己压力。你高中的最后几个月就过得无忧无虑的，因为那时几乎没什么压力可言，大学也已经申请下来了。但最近这几周里，我们注意到你又开始烦乱（知道你紧张时会咬指甲吗？）。没什么好担心的。唯一重要的是你用心学了，而唯一可以用来衡量的标准就是你努力与否。分数只是些愚蠢的数字罢了，虚荣的人可以籍此吹嘘，而懒惰的人却要为此恐慌。你如此优秀，不会沦为这两种人。

最重要的是要广交朋友，乐观开朗。大学时代的朋友往往是你一生中最值得珍惜的，因为大学四年你和他们朝夕相处，亲过家人。同时，

bonding experience. Pick a few friends and become really close to them—pick the ones who are genuine and sincere to you. Don't worry about their hobbies, grades, looks, or even personalities. You have developed some real friendships in high school in your last two years, so trust your instinct, and make new friends. You are a genuine and sincere person—anyone would enjoy being your friend, so be confident, outgoing, and pro-active. If you think you like someone, tell her. You have very little to lose. Give people the benefit of the doubt; don't stereotype; and be forgiving. People are not perfect, so as long as they are genuine and sincere, trust them and be good to them. They will give back. This is my secret of success—that I am genuine with people and trust them (unless they do something to lose my trust). Some people tell me that occasionally I would be taken advantage of. They are right, but I can tell you that that loss is nothing compared to what I gained. In my last 18 years leading people, I have realized that only one thing matters—to gain the trust and respect of others, and to do so, you need to trust and respect others first. Whether it is for management, work, or friendship, this is something you should **ponder**[①].

Do keep your high school friends, and stay connected to them, but do not use them as substitutes for college friendship, and do not spend too much time with them, because that would eat into your time to make new friends.

Start planning for your summers early—what would you like to do? Where would you like to live? What would you like to learn? What have you

① ponder ['pɒndə] v. 沉思，考虑；回想，反思

一起学会独立，一起长大成人，这种经历自然会将你们紧密相连。结交几个真诚的朋友，用心相待，别在意他们的喜好、学业、外在甚至是个性。你在高中的后两年里已经交到了一些真心的朋友，所以尽管相信自己的直觉，去结识新的朋友吧。你本真诚，任何人都会乐于跟你做朋友的，所以在交往中要自信、外向、主动一点。如果你感觉自己喜欢谁，就坦率告诉她，你也没什么可损失的。从善意的角度看待他人的行为，不要存成见，要宽容大度。人无完人，只要他们够真诚，你就要信任他们，友善待之，他们必将回报于你。这亦是我成功的秘诀——坦诚相见，信赖他人（除非他们做了失信于我的事）。有人告诉我说，我偶尔会被人利用了。他们说得对，但是我可以告诉你，那点损失和我得到的相比根本不算什么。在我过去 18 年的领导生涯里，我意识到了重要的一点，那就是，要赢得他人的信任和尊重；而要做到这一点，你首先就要信任和尊重他人。因此，无论是在管理还是在工作中，抑或是与他人建立友谊，这一点都值得你深思。

不要断绝你高中时代的朋友，同他们保持联系。但不要让他们取代你大学阶段的友谊，也不要把时间过多地花在这些老朋友身上，否则你就没空结交新朋友了。

早点开始规划你的暑期安排——想做什么？想呆在哪？想学点什么吗？有没有大学里学到的哪样东西能转变你的思想？我觉得你打算学时

learned in college that might change your mind? I think your plan of studying fashion is good, and you should decide where you want to be, and get into the right courses. We of course hope you come back to Beijing, but you should go where you think is best for you.

Whether it is summer-planning, or coursework planning, or picking a major, or managing your time, you should take control of your life. In the past, I have helped you quite a bit, whether it is in college applications, designing your **extracurricular**[①] activities, or picking the initial coursework. I will always be there for you, but the time has come for you to be in the driver's seat—this is your life, and you need to be in control. I will always remember the exhilarating feeling in my life—that I got to decide to skip kindergarten, that I got to decide to change to computer science major, that I got to decide to leave academia for Apple, that I got to decide to go to China, that I got to decide to go to Google, and most recently, that I got to decide to start my own business. Being able to decide means you get to live the life that you want to. Life is too short to live the life others do or others want you to. Being in control feels great. Try it, and you'll love it!

I told your mom I'm writing this letter, and asked what she wanted me to say. She thought and said: "just ask her to take care of herself." Simple but deeply caring—that is how your mother is, and that is why you love her so much. In this simple sentence is her hope that you will become independent in the way you take care of yourself—that you will remember to take your

① extracurricular ['ɛkstrəkə'rikjələ] adj. 学校课程以外的

尚设计的想法就很不错，你应该想好去哪里学，并选好相应的课程。我们当然希望你能回北京来，但你还是应该去你最想去的地方。

不管是暑期计划，课程规划，选择专业，还是时间管理，你都要把握住自己。过去，无论是申请大学，策划课外活动，还是选择初始课程，我都不断地从旁指点你。我会一直守护你，但现在该是你自己掌舵的时候了——你自己的人生，要自己来作主。我总能回想起人生中那些个令人振奋的时刻——决定不上幼儿园，决定转修计算机专业，决定离开学术界转投苹果公司，决定回国发展，决定任职谷歌，乃至最近决定创办我自己的公司。有抉择力意味着你将开始过自己想要的人生。人生苦短，不应随波逐流或为他人过活。我的人生我作主是一种非凡的体验。去尝试吧，你会喜欢的！

我告诉你妈妈我在写这封信，问她有什么想对你说的话。她想了想，说："让她照顾好自己。"言简而情深，这才是你的妈妈，亦是你深爱她的原因。千言万语都饱含在这短短的一句话里，她寄望于你能通过照顾自己学会如何独立生活——她想提醒你要按时吃药，注意休息，合理膳食，适量运动，不舒服时一定记得去看医生。中国有句古话："身体发肤，受之父母，不敢毁伤，孝之始也。"（意思是说，孝敬父母最好的方

medicine, that you will get enough sleep, that you will have a balanced diet, that you will get some exercise, and that you will go see a doctor whenever you don't feel good. An ancient Chinese proverb says that the most important thing to be nice to your parents is to take care of yourself. This is because your parents love you so much, and that if you are well, they will have comfort. You will understand this one day when you become a mother. But in the meantime, please listen to your mother and take care of yourself.

College is the four years where you have:

• the greatest amount of free time

• the first chance to be independent

• the most flexibility to change

• the lowest risk for making mistakes

So please treasure your college years—make the best of your free time, become an independent thinker in control of your destiny, evolve yourself into a bi-cultural talent, be bold to experiment, learn and grow through your successes and challenges.

When I faced the greatest challenge and opportunity in my life in 2005, you gave me a big hug and said "bonne chance", which means "good luck" and "good courage". Now I do the same for you. Bonne chance, my angel and princess. May Columbia become the happiest four years in your life, and may you blossom into just what you dream to be.

Love,

Dad (& Mom)

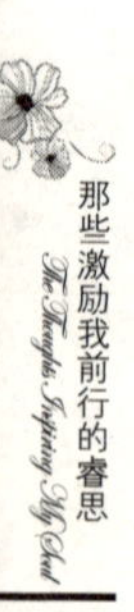

式就是爱护自己，因为父母如此爱你，你一切都好，他们也就安心了。）等你为人之母时就会深谙其意了。与此同时，听你妈妈的话，好好照顾自己。

大学这四年里你将：

· 最大限度地拥有自由时间

· 第一次有机会独立生活

· 处于可塑性最强的阶段

· 从错误中获取教训的代价最小

所以，珍惜你的大学时光吧——充分利用你的自由时间，成为能独立思考来掌控自身命运的人，把自己发展成学贯中西的人才，大胆去尝试，在成功与挑战中不断学习和成长。

当我在2005年面临人生中最大的挑战与机遇时，你给了我一个大大的拥抱，用法文“Bonne Chance”来鼓励我，这句话代表着“好运”与“坚强”。现在我要对你说同样的话，Bonne Chance，我的天使我的公主。愿哥伦比亚大学的四年成为你人生中最快乐的时光，祝你成长为你梦想的那个你！

爱你的，

爸爸（携妈妈）

What matters is not the idea a man holds,

but the depth at which he holds it.

重要的不是思想，

而是思想的深度。